POWER READING

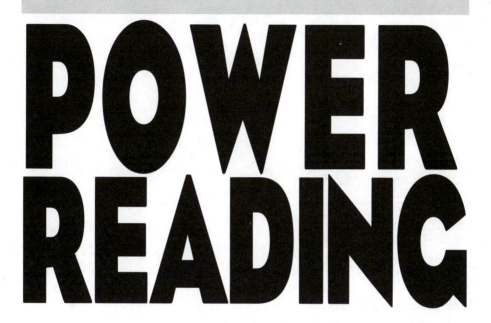

Laurie Rozakis, Ph.D.

Macmillan • USA

Macmillan General Reference
A Simon & Schuster Macmillan Company
1633 Broadway
New York, NY 10019

An Arco Book

MACMILLAN is a registered trademark of Macmillan, Inc.
ARCO is a registered trademark of Prentice-Hall, Inc.

Library of Congress Cataloging-in-Publication Data

Rozakis, Laurie.
    Power reading / Laurie Rozakis.
        p.   cm.
    ISBN 0-02-860562-4
    1.   Speed reading.   I.   Title.
  LB1050.54.R69   1995
  418' .4--dc20   95-34428
                    CIP

Manufactured in the United States of America
10 9 8 7 6 5 4 3 2 1

To my father, Werner Joseph Neu,
who helped teach me to read and
to understand

Contents

Introduction

Why Power Reading Is a Necessity

Information Overload

The Information Age is upon us—and there's no escape! Ready or not, we are in the midst of the greatest explosion of information the world has ever seen. No other age has been blitzed by the data, reports, details, examples, opinions, statistics, and facts that we are exposed to daily—and futurists guarantee that this onslaught of information will only increase. Consider these facts about information today:

- *One daily edition* of *The New York Times* contains more information than an educated sixteenth-century person assimilated in his entire lifetime.

- *Fifty thousand books* are published in the United States every year.

- *Ten thousand magazines* are currently published in the United States.

- *Seven thousand scientific studies* are written daily worldwide.

- More information has been produced in the *last fifty years* than in the previous *five thousand.*

- Today, the amount of information available doubles *every five years.*

- By the year 2000, the amount of information available will double in *less than two years!*

There is so much information that even the huge Library of Congress fears the deluge. The library now holds more than 100 million items. To deal with the influx of new information, the library has announced an ambitious plan to convert into digital form, by the year 2000, all the most important materials in its collection and in the collections of all public and research libraries. The new collection, called the National Digital Library, will become the most extensive source of material for the National Information Infrastructure, the so-called Information Superhighway. Here's how it will work:

1. About 1 million documents will be digitized each year.

2. Included will be books, photographs, paintings, and videos.

3. Users can access materials through modems, cable, and satellite TV.

4. Cross-referencing allows users to click on highlighted terms and access multiple documents or libraries.

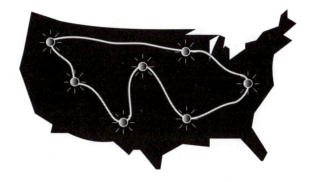

Welcome to the Future!

Information is being produced so quickly that professionals—computer specialists, engineers, researchers, scientists—will have to be reeducated every decade. People in cutting-edge technologies likely will find their skills outmoded in less than half that time. No one is exempt: The day when you could earn a college degree and then relax with your skills is a thing of the past.

Studies show that the average business professional is required to read at least *4 million words per month*—that's *50 million words a year!* In the medical profession alone, more than ten thousand professional journals are published yearly.

And what about the materials people want to read for pleasure or information? When is there time for novels, magazines, newspapers, and poetry? If you are like most people, the newspapers, magazines, and books pile up everywhere until you feel compelled to throw everything out to make room for more current materials.

The Effect of the Electronic Revolution

The electronic revolution has added to this onslaught of information. Technology, which promised to simplify the flow of information and make it more manageable, has had just the opposite effect. PC workstations, laptops, computer notebooks, CD-ROMs, videos, fiber optics and satellites have made it possible to transmit volumes of information in an instant. For example, it is now possible to transmit a year's worth of the *New York Times* in seconds.

The computer revolution has not reduced the amount of paper generated in the average office, however. According to one estimate, paper use has increased more than six times with the advent of the electronic office. What's the result? We are barraged by an unprecedented amount of information and there is just not enough time to deal with it all.

New Realities

Our world is being changed in exciting—and frightening—ways. The Information Age promises to bring radical changes in the ways we work, live, and even think. One of the most profound changes is the amount of information we face and the way we process it.

All this information has radically changed the nature of the marketplace. Increasingly, what counts now is how well people think. According to the latest projections, by the beginning of the twenty-first century nearly half of all service workers will be involved in collecting, storing, and analyzing information. The people who get ahead in the Information Age will be those who are able to assimilate chunks of information quickly and accurately, sorting necessary facts, examples, and details from unnecessary material.

Information Anxiety

People have become contemporary versions of the Greek mythological figure Sisyphus, who was fated to spend eternity pushing a huge rock up a hill in Hades only to have it tumble back down right before he reached the crest. What is today's rock? Information.

There doesn't seem to be a way to keep the information from getting the better of us. No matter how hard you push, you can't seem to keep up with all the written words pouring down. Writer Richard Saul Wurman has named this feeling of frustration *information anxiety*. It's the feeling of tension you get when you look at the overflowing stacks of newspapers, the desk piled high with papers, the shelves of new books in the library, the rows of un-familiar magazines on the newsstand.

Take this quiz to see if you are a victim of Information Anxiety.

Information Anxiety Quiz

Directions: Circle Yes or No for each question.

Yes No **1.** Do you think it is important to keep up with current events?

Yes No **2.** Do you have trouble reading all the information you need for your job?

Yes No **3.** Is your desk piled high with unread memos, letters, reports, and faxes?

Yes No **4.** Is it important that you keep up with the latest information in your field?

Yes No **5.** Do you have to take work home from the office to get through your paperwork?

Yes No **6.** Do you feel tense about getting through all the reading you have to do?

Yes No **7.** Do you get at least ten newspapers and magazines a week?

Yes No **8.** Do you have trouble finding time to read all the newspapers and magazines you get?

Yes No **9.** Do you read all the information you get in the mail?

Yes No **10.** Do you sometimes feel that you are not getting the most from what you are reading?

Yes No **11.** Does your mind wander as you read?

Yes No **12.** Do you find yourself rereading passages?

Yes No **13.** Do you wish that you had the time for some pleasure reading?

Yes No **14.** Do you wish that you could read faster?

Yes No **15.** Do you wish you could remember more of what you read?

Yes No **16.** Do you envy people who can read quickly and accurately?

If you circled "yes" six or more times, this book can help you!

Speed Reading: The Key to Success in the Information Age

It's no secret that how well you read can affect your career. Keeping up with the latest information can be the key to professional and personal success. The better your reading skills, the more pleasure you will derive from reading. A person who likes to read always has a friend—a book!

If you can double or even triple your reading rate you can save yourself two or more hours a day. Your increased productivity can save your company thousands of dollars a year, and free you up to act on the new knowledge you have acquired and processed. There is now a way to manage the onslaught of information, and it's not as difficult as you may think: Learn Power Reading.

Power Reading is a proven way to help you master the skills you need to read more quickly and accurately. You will learn to read for all your needs: information, business, pleasure, and test-taking. There's no preparation, either—all you need is the desire to read faster and better and a few minutes each day. One of the best dividends of learning Power Reading is that it requires just a small commitment of time to produce rich rewards. Spend just fifteen minutes each day with this book and soon you will have the tools you need to master your reading load.

Think about the little parcels of time that are otherwise wasted. Use the time you spend waiting in line at the bus stop, sitting in a dentist's office, or tapping your heel as you wait for a late appointment. Use this time to help you acquire skills that will last a lifetime. Remember, Power Reading can help you

◆ read faster

◆ think better

◆ learn quickly

◆ retain more

◆ focus better

◆ enjoy more

◆ relax more

How to Use This Book

People approach books in different ways. Some people plunge right in and work directly from the beginning to the end. Others skim and pick and choose the lessons that they find the most appealing. Still others start at the middle and read to the end, flipping to the front if they feel a little guilty. The way you read a book depends on your purpose for reading, and different methods work better with different kinds of books. In order to get the maximum benefit from *Power Reading,* here's the method we recommend.

1. Check out the table of contents!

   ◆ Pay special attention to the table of contents.

   ◆ Read it through carefully to understand what material the book contains and how everything is organized.

   ◆ Make sure you understand the structure of the book before you go on.

2. Don't forget the Introduction!

   ◆ Read the Introduction.

   ◆ Focus on the information it contains.

   ◆ See what new information you can gather about the book from the introduction.

3. Skim the book.

   ◆ Flip through the entire book.

   ◆ See how the chapters and lessons are arranged.

   ◆ Note the way the pages are laid out.

   ◆ Locate any special features, such as illustrations, charts, or appendices.

4. Set up a Power Reading schedule.

   ◆ Allocate a specific amount of time every day. We recommend fifteen minutes daily, in one segment.

◆ If possible, stick to the same time period every day. For example, try to complete a section before work, from 7:00 to 7:15 A.M. Or use some time during lunch, say 12:00 to 12:15. Early evening is also a good time to work. Try 8:00 to 8:15 P.M. or 8:30 to 8:45. Don't wait until too late at night or you will be too tired to concentrate clearly.

◆ Stick to the schedule!

Here's a sample schedule you can use to keep track of your progress.

Date	Time	Number of Pages	Topics Learned

Part 1

Power Reading Basics

He has only half learned the art of reading who has not added to it the even more refined accomplishments of skipping and skimming.

—Arthur Balfour

Test Your Reading Speed

The art of reading is extremely important. It consists in our not taking up whatever happens to occupy the larger public.

—Arthur Schopenhauer

Reading is a process by which our minds translate symbols into ideas. How quickly you are able to decode and process this information is your reading speed and comprehension level. Before you can begin to learn Power Reading, however, it is essential to know the rate at which you read and how much of the material you absorb. You will use these scores as benchmarks to judge your progress throughout this book. Tests are provided throughout to track your mastery of Power Reading techniques.

Take the tests in optimal surroundings. Make sure that you sit comfortably, have good reading light, and have no distractions.

A Note on Timing

Accurate timing is crucial. As you begin to Power Read, you will need to keep track of your progress by comparing your different reading scores. Don't be discouraged if these scores vary widely at first; prior knowledge about the reading material and personal feelings about the subject can all affect your reading rate. Over a period of weeks, however, you should see significant gains in reading speed and comprehension, and consistency in your scores.

To time your reading, use an ordinary clock or watch with a sweep second hand. If you wish, you can use a stopwatch, kitchen timer, or alarm clock—all work extremely well for your purpose here. Start reading just as the second hand reaches 12. Be sure to note the exact time and *write it down*. Don't try to remember the starting time; this will merely serve to distract you from reading, slow you down, and impede comprehension. Then recheck the clock or watch when you finish reading. Immediately write down the time, in minutes and seconds.

Determining Your Reading Rate

To figure out how fast you read, follow these easy steps:

1. Set up your clock or timer as described above.

2. Start reading.

3. After one minute, stop reading.

4. Note the number of the line where you have stopped reading.

5. Multiply that number by 10 (the average number of words per line).

6. This is your initial reading speed.

Below is your test. See how well you do.

 Women and Business

1   The Small Business Administration supports women-owned businesses,

2   recognizing that they remain one of the fastest growing sectors of the

3   economy and that women continue to start businesses at twice the rate

4   of men. The United States Census Bureau statistics indicate that women

5   currently own 32 percent of the small businesses in the United States;

6   they estimate that this figure will likely jump to 40 percent—or even

7   higher—by the year 2000.

8   Despite advancements, however, women continue to face unique

9   challenges in business. In light of this, the Small Business Administration

10   offers a range of resources to assist women entrepreneurs in starting and

11   expanding their businesses through the Office of Women's Business

12   Ownership. These programs address the challenges presented by women

13   business owners and offer specially designed programs to help them

14   overcome obstacles.

15   Among the most successful of the new programs is one that involves

16   having women in business team up with a mentor—a woman entrepreneur

17 who has been in business longer, faced similar challenges, found

18 solutions, and wants to share what she has learned, one-to-one, with

19 someone in the process of starting a business of her own.

20 The Small Business Administration recognizes the need to provide

21 women business owners with this kind of help. Consequently, in 1988,

22 the Small Business Administration's Office of Women's Business

23 Ownership developed a new program: the Women's Network for

24 Entrepreneurial Training (WNET).

26 WNET is designed to match successful women entrepreneurs (mentors)

27 with women business owners (protégés) whose companies are ready to

28 grow. For a period of one year, the mentor serves as a role model and

29 offers technical assistance. According to Lindsay Johnson, director of

30 the Office of Women's Business Ownership, "In the mentors, we

31 discovered a wealth of expert knowledge about when we take risks,

32 experiment, diversify, expand, or conserve. And we're proud to say that

33 our protégés have used that experience to help their businesses flourish."

34 What are some of the benefits of being a mentor or protégé? "It feels

35 good to help another person by looking back on my own progress and

36 sharing my experience," says Masaka Tani Boissonnault, a mentor who is

37 the cofounder of Arch-I-Form, a Los Angeles company. "I have a special

38 camaraderie with my mentor," comments Wendy Blazed, a protégé who

39 created Edible Style in Los Angeles. "I came away from my first meeting

40 with dozens of marketing ideas. And she's helping me get past the fear

41 factor. The whole thing is very inspiring." Marsha Durban, a mentor from

42 East Rutherford, New Jersey, who created the firm of Technolog, Inc., is

43 equally enthusiastic. "I've learned so much from my protégé. As I give

44 her advice, I realize I should be applying that same advice to my own

45 issues. It helps me put my business in perspective."

46 Who can be a mentor? Any woman business owner who:

47 ◆ founded her company and has been its CEO for at least five years

48 ◆ has a successful business, demonstrated by steady growth of

49 her company

50 ◆ is willing to devote an average of four hours per month to her

51 protégé for at least one year

52   ◆ is willing, on a one-to-one basis with her protégé, to discuss and provide

53   necessary information about business in order to assist in developing a

54   mentor relationship.

55   Who can be a protégé? The opportunity is open to any woman business

56   owner who:

57   ◆ has been in business for at least one year and is ready to take a growth

58   step that involves some risk

59   ◆ demonstrates strong entrepreneurial skills and shows potential for

60   continued business success in her chosen business field

61   ◆ is willing to spend an average of four hours a month with her mentor

62   receiving guidance, training, and counseling

63   ◆ demonstrates a willingness to apply the advice she receives from her

64   mentor to her business.

65   The Office of Women's Business Ownership was created to meet the

66   needs of the increasing numbers of new women business owners and help

67   them join the community of successful entrepreneurs. Through a national

68   network of local Small Business Administration offices, the Office of

69   Women's Business Owners offers potential and established women

70   entrepreneurs a range of services and resources that include

71   pre-business workshops, "Access to Capital" conferences, technical and

72   financial information, an extensive national data base, procurement

73   conferences, how to sell to the federal government seminars, exporting

74   conferences, and long-term training and counseling centers set up in

75   partnership with private companies. The Small Business Administration

76   offices around the country can be found in the telephone directory under

77   the U.S. Government listings. Each office has an Office of Women's

78   Business Ownership representative who will be happy to talk with you

79   about the program.

80   "It is around small businesses that you find communities growing and

81   prospering. It is where women and minorities make their mark as

82   business owners. Thousands of these business are aiding those in need

83   all across the country right now," says one highly successful

84   entrepreneur.

Now figure out your reading speed.

Example: You stopped reading on line 18.

Multiply 18 × 10.

Your initial reading speed is: 180 words per minute.

I stopped reading on line:_____

line number_____ × 10 =_____

initial reading speed is:_____

Reading Rates

500–1500 words per minute	*Power Reader*
250 words per minute	Average reader
150 words per minute	Average speaker

How to Use Your Score

Don't be discouraged if you're not a Power Reader. At this point, you are very likely reading at about a quarter of your maximum ability. This means that more than three-quarters of your ability remains unused!

Remember: Power Readers use different reading speeds for different tasks. You will, too, after you complete this book. For example, you might read the newspaper at 1200 words per minute, a magazine at 1000 words per minute, and a memo or letter at 800 words per minute. But if the material is more technical, you will adjust your reading rate to compensate. For a technical manual, for example, you might read at no more than 700 words per minute. This book will teach you how to combine speed and comprehension.

Measuring Everyday Reading

The reports, memos, and faxes on your desk do not have numbered lines running down one side. How can you measure your reading rate under everyday reading situations when the length, variety, and difficulty of the material varies? We recommend this method:

1. Count the number of words in the first six lines.
   Example: 60 words

2. Divide this by 6 to give you the number of words per line.
   Example: 10 words

3. Multiply this number by the number of lines per page.
   Example: 10 words × 50 = 500 words

4. Multiply this by the number of pages you read.
   Example: 500 words × 10 pages = 5000 words

5. Subtract your starting time from your ending time.
   Example: 2:05 – 2:00 = 5 minutes

6. Divide the number of words by the reading time.
   Example: 5000 words ÷ 5 minutes = 1000 words per minute

Use the above method to calculate your rate for the next passage.

Toxic New World

**What Nurses Can Do to Cope with a
Polluted Environment**

Late one winter's afternoon as some nurses were taking their break, they were startled to see the hospital exterminator unexpectedly come down their wing, spraying casually and indiscriminately around desks and chairs. Within seconds, a fine mist of choking fumes was settling on their coffee and donuts.

After a few minutes the exterminator was gone, leaving a stunned group of nurses and their untouched snacks. The nurses began to talk among themselves, concerned about the effects of spraying, year-in and year-out. One related her knowledge of a local family forced from their home because of misapplied pesticides. Others spoke of the helpless, elderly patients one floor below in the acute medical-surgical wing. These patients could not move or get up to open their windows when the exterminator came.

Worried, the nurses called the supervisor of Work Control, who assured them that there was "no danger … well, maybe just a little headache for a while." The nurses, knowing that "a little headache" could be central nervous system toxicity, called the local poison control center. The center informed them that the pesticide used by their hospital carried a manufacturer's warning that the sprayed area should be evacuated for four to five hours, or until the foul odor disappeared. The side effects, they were told, were CNS toxicity.

Armed with this knowledge, the nurses telephoned Work Control and requested that the guidelines be followed, especially in areas containing helpless patients. After some initial reluctance (and some judiciously applied pressure by the local nurses' union), the building was sprayed, using the necessary precautions.

In the following months, Work Control realized that the nurses were very interested in a safe, hygienic, nontoxic work environment. During this time, issues of asbestos dust (from the installation of a new telephone system) and methane gas (seeping into the building from air shafts) came into discussion as well.

Nurses, such as those in this hospital, are finding that among the emerging new images of the nurse in the 1990s is that of the concerned, aware, and active health-care provider in a silent epidemic. Meanwhile, the public is ignorant of the toxicity of our present-day environment. Most people feel that environmental toxins affect only veterans of the Vietnam War (Agent Orange), coal miners (silicosis), ghetto children (lead poisoning), or nuclear power-plant workers (radiation poisoning). Occasionally, newspaper articles appear about families who are victims of gasoline spills or inept exterminators. In general, people read these stories and have only a moment's concern or pity, sure that what they have just read is only an isolated instance. This is an illusion: The toxic effects of a post-industrial society pollute our environment more than most of us are willing to acknowledge.

Our Toxic Environment

Fresh-water fish specimens prior to 1940 were virtually free from gonadal tumors, and only 1 percent of the fish had any type of cancer. Today, many waterways are polluted by industrial waste products. Such places as the Niagara River, the Buffalo River, the Hudson River estuary, the Black River in Ohio, Chesapeake Bay, Yaquia Bay in Oregon, Puget Sound, and the Great Lakes now have a large population of cancerous fish. Scientists, working under exacting conditions, have painted laboratory fish with the polluted slime from the bottom of these waterways. They found that these fish developed cancer, too.

Rising cancer rates in such places as New Jersey and Nassau County, New York, have prompted researchers to study these areas. Findings from a four-year study by the National Cancer Institute show that there is a correlation between New Jersey's status as a chemical manufacturing center and its high incidence of cancer. The New York State Department of Environmental Conservation has deplored the fouling of Long Island's underground water by industrial wastes and agricultural pesticides, and the destruction of the Pine Barrens, an island-wide stretch of pine forest that helps ensure a pure water table.

Behavioral scientists are also involved. Recently, they have begun to see their field as an environmental health science. That is partly due to evidence that normal physiological and sociological development is affected by low-level environmental toxins. The effects are often so subtle as to be easily missed or dismissed. As psychologists study the problem, signs of chronic exposure to overtly asymptomatic toxins begin to emerge: a slightly lower birth size; an increase in miscarriages and birth defects; increased fatigue, irritability, and dyslexia in children; skin and respiratory problems; and severe migraine headaches.

Action Guidelines for Nurses

Nurses and other health care givers are increasingly concerned about the detection and prevention of disease caused by environmental pollution. Some will wish to work with researchers, special interest groups, and support groups. Several guidelines are offered below to those who want to add their expertise to solving the problem of our environment:

◆ Be willing to admit to the idea of asymptomatic, subclinical toxicity and the multiple-effects disease model.

◆ Be aware that environmental toxicology is a politically charged issue, involving the world of high finance, entrenched interests, and corporate ego.

◆ Be able to accept disbelief, and even anger, toward not only the message but also the messenger.

◆ Be aware that some researchers tend toward insularity, skepticism, and professional jealously about the work of others in their field.

◆ Be willing to use assessment of behavioral functions as a total for evaluating subclinical toxicity.

◆ Be aware that almost no research on the synergistic effects of low-level toxins has been done, with the consequence of down-playing its importance.

When the nurses referred to in the beginning of this article were trying to solve the problem of insecticide spraying in the hospital, they faced stiff opposition. Despite their professionalism and valid concerns, they met with disbelief from their supervisor, anger from Work Control, and unidentified threatening telephone calls regarding their actions. They found both their union and the local poison control center supportive and informative. However, researchers at the nearby university were skeptical. They found their coworkers at first alarmed at the prospect of toxicity through low-level exposure to the pesticide. Soon these same coworkers doubted their concerns, as no immediate effects could be detected. Conflicting information, lack of information, denial, and anger are all problems that can hinder attempts to protect the environment.

Conclusions

There are several coping mechanisms that will help counteract the above problems. Knowledge is the primary one. Medical and scientific journals can be researched for information on pollutants, toxicity levels, recent findings on side effects, and laboratory studies. Newspapers can be used to pinpoint the specific concerns of the community. Unions, usually alert to protecting the worker and maintaining a healthy work environment, can be sources of information on health problems. Poison control centers are good places for validating information on pollutants, especially pesticides. A study of the history of the land of your home and workplace is the next step. Being aware of what surrounds you (industry, airports, highways, waste areas, etc.) may give clues to the potential for environmental poisoning.

Research of this type will results in lists of individuals and organizations for sharing information, and can provide the basis for forming action groups. The health care giver may also wish to start educating the community about the effects of low levels of pollution. Any facts collected could be useful to local environmental groups.

Our toxic world need not be so. The Frankenstein monster of overdevelopment and misuse of technology can be turned back. There is a chance that change can—that change must—come about. Concerned, informed, and active health care givers can play a responsible part in ensuring environmental safety for their patients, ourselves, our children, and, ultimately, the future health of the human race.

Calculate Your Reading Speed

1. Count the number of words in the first six lines. _____

2. Divide this number by 6. _____

3. Multiply this by the number of lines per page. _____

4. Multiply this by the number of pages you read. _____

5. Subtract your starting time from your ending time._____

6. Divide the number of words by the reading time. _____

   Reading speed: _____

In the next chapter, you will learn specific ways to increase your reading speed and comprehension.

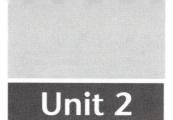

Unit 2

Test Your Reading Comprehension

I took a course in speed reading and was able to read War and Peace *in twenty minutes. It's about Russia.*

—*Woody Allen*

Power Reading is more than reading fast—it's understanding what you read. To deal with the extraordinary amount of reading generated by the Information Age, you must not only read fast; you must also accurately comprehend the meaning behind the words. How well do you grasp what you read?

Below are three sample passages you can use to rate your reading comprehension. Read each passage and answer the questions that follow.

Allow yourself fifteen minutes for each passage. You may find that you cannot finish in the fifteen minutes. Keep track of your time, determine your reading speed, and see if you find yourself working faster by the final passage. Then check the answer key to see how well you understood the point of each passage by inferring and analyzing what you read.

1: Firearms and Violence

Approximately 60 percent of all murder victims in the United States in 1989 (about twelve thousand people) were killed with firearms. According to estimates, firearm attacks injured another seventy thousand victims, some of whom were left permanently disabled. In 1985 the cost of shootings—either by others, through self-inflicted wounds, or in accidents—was estimated to be more than $14 billion nationwide for medical care, long-term disability, and premature death. Among firearms, handguns are the murder weapon of choice. While handguns make up only one third of all firearms owned in the United States, they account for 80 percent of all murders committed with firearms.

Teenagers and young adults face especially high risks of being murdered with a firearm. Figures for 1990 from the National Center for Health Statistics indicate that 82 percent of all murder victims aged fifteen to nineteen and 76 percent of victims aged twenty to twenty-four were killed with guns. The risk was especially high for black males in those age ranges. The firearm murder rate was 105.3 per 100,000 black males aged fifteen to nineteen, compared to 9.7 for white males in the same age group. This 11:1 ratio of black-to-white rates reflects a perplexing increase since 1985, when the firearm rate for black males aged fifteen to nineteen was 37.4 per 100,000. Among twenty- to twenty-four-year-old black males, the rate increased from 63.2 to 140.7. For several years before 1985, the rates for black males in these age groups had been decreasing. The recent increases have not been paralleled for females, nor have they been matched in nonmurder rates or even firearm suicide rates for young black males. (The latter are higher among whites than among blacks but have risen recently for both races.)

Any firearm murder follows a particular chain of events: One person acquires a firearm; two or more people come within reach of the firearm; a dispute escalates into an attack; the weapon is fired and it causes an injury; and the injury is serious enough to cause death. While that sequence probably seems obvious, thinking about gun murders as a chain of events draws attention to a series of risks that should be measured and questions that should be considered in designing strategies to reduce murders or other violent events that involve guns.

Speculation about the relationship between gun availability and violence takes two directions. On one hand, greater availability of guns may deter potential perpetrators of violent crimes out of fear that the intended victim may be armed. On the other hand, greater availability of guns may encourage people who are contemplating committing a violent crime to carry it out but first to arm themselves to overcome their fear of retaliation. Greater gun availability may also increase violence levels if guns that are kept at home or in cars are stolen during burglaries, enter illegal markets, and encourage criminals to attack victims they would pass up without being armed. Guns kept in homes may also be used in family arguments that might have ended nonviolently if guns were not available.

How are these conflicting speculations resolved in actual practice? The best way to answer this question would be to measure violent crime levels before and after an intervention that substantially reduced gun availability. However, opportunities to evaluate the effects of such interventions have arisen in only a few jurisdictions. As a result, researchers have used four less powerful approaches to study how gun availability affects violence and its consequences. Their findings, while somewhat tentative and not entirely consistent, nonetheless suggest that greater gun availability increases murder rates and influences the choice of weapon in violent crimes but does not affect overall levels of nonfatal violence.

Although available data on how guns are obtained are fragmented and outdated, they suggest that illegal or unregulated transactions are the primary source of guns used in violence. For example, only 29 percent of 113 guns used in felonies committed in Boston during 1976 were bought directly from federally licensed gun dealers. Between the manufacturer and the criminal user, 20 percent of the guns passed through a chain of unregulated private transfers, while 40 percent were stolen. Most of the illegal suppliers found in this sample were small-scale independent operators who sold only a few guns per month, rather than large organizations or licensed dealers working largely off the books.

> Reading Time: _____
>
> Word Count: 570
>
> Reading Speed: _____

Directions: Answer the following questions on the basis of the passage you just read. You may look back as often as necessary to find the correct answer. For each question, underline the answer you think is best.

1. How many people were killed by firearms in 1989?
   (A) 60
   (B) 70,000
   (C) between 10,000 and 14,000
   (D) fewer than 10,000

2. According to this passage, why are handguns so dangerous?
- (A) Although they are among the least often purchased firearms, they cause a disproportionate number of deaths.
- (B) They cost the least to buy, which makes them the most popular weapons.
- (C) They are used most often for self-inflicted wounds.
- (D) Teenagers and young adults find them easily available.

3. Which people are at the highest risk for dying violently?
- (A) black women
- (B) people aged 13 to 21
- (C) middle-aged black males
- (D) teenagers and women

4. How many steps are involved in a murder by handgun?
- (A) two
- (B) four
- (C) three
- (D) five

5. Which statement is true, according to the information in this passage?
- (A) There is a clear-cut relationship between the availability of handguns and murder rates.
- (B) The easy availability of guns encourages violent crimes.
- (C) There is no simple relationship between the availability of guns and the number of murders committed with them every year.
- (D) Guns should never be kept at home because they can be used in family arguments.

6. Researchers have tentatively concluded that
- (A) guns must be restricted to save lives
- (B) they need to use less powerful approaches to solve this problem
- (C) gun availability does not affect murder rates
- (D) greater gun availability does not affect the overall number of gun accidents

7. Research suggests that guns most often find their ways into people's hands by
- (A) legal means
- (B) violent acts
- (C) illegal means
- (D) outdated methods

8. Illegal suppliers of guns are most often
   (A) large organizations
   (B) small shop owners
   (C) licensed dealers
   (D) family members

9. The best heading for the last paragraph in this selection would be
   (A) How do people obtain possession of the guns they use in violent crimes?
   (B) How is gun availability related to violence levels?
   (C) Does the use of a gun in self-defense reduce the chance of an injury?
   (D) How are criminals cornering the market on illegal weapons?

10. The author of this passage would most likely agree with which of the following statements?
   (A) All guns must be banned at once.
   (B) Guns are becoming an increasingly serious problem for all Americans.
   (C) If teenagers and young adults were taught how to correctly handle firearms, the murder and accident rate would decrease drastically.
   (D) Banning guns is not the solution to our problem; rather, we must institute social and economic programs among the disadvantaged.

Answers

1. (C)	3. (B)	5. (C)	7. (C)	9. (A)
2. (A)	4. (D)	6. (D)	8. (B)	10. (B)

The Moment of Truth: How Did You Do?

Excellent readers	9–10 correct
Above-average readers	7–8 correct
Average readers	5–6 correct
Below-average readers	less than 4 correct

2: Electric Energy

America's electric utilities are finding that helping their customers use energy more efficiently can be a cost-effective and reliable alternative for meeting electricity demand growth. The opportunities for efficiency improvements are myriad and potential savings real, but consumers and utilities have been slow to invest in the most cost-effective energy-efficient technologies available.

The energy efficiency of today's buildings and electric equipment and appliances falls far short of what is technically available. This efficiency gap has been attributed to a variety of market, institutional, technical, and behavioral constraints. Electric utility energy-efficiency programs have great potential to narrow this gap and achieve significant energy savings.

Utilities' energy-efficiency programs also promise savings for consumers and utilities, profits for shareholders, improvements in industrial productivity, enhanced international competitiveness, and reduced environmental impacts. But along with opportunities, greater reliance on energy efficiency as a resource to meet future electricity needs also entails risks—that efficient technologies will not perform as well as promised, that anticipated savings will not be truly cost effective in practice, and that the costs and benefits of energy-efficiency programs will not be shared equitably among utility customers.

In 1992, utility power generation accounted for 36 percent of total primary energy use in the United States, and electricity consumption is growing faster than overall energy use. Current growth forecasts range from 1 to 3.5 percent per year over the next decade. Meeting this new demand could require construction of the equivalent of 50 to 220 new 1,000-megawatt power plants over 10 years. The differences in estimated new capacity needs reflect hundreds of billions of dollars for utility rate payers. Of course, future electricity demand growth rates are uncertain, adding to the risks that utilities face in planning and building for the future.

Energy-efficiency advocates have long maintained that it can be cheaper for rate payers and better for the environment and society to save energy rather than build new power plants. This view is now embraced by many utilities, regulators, shareholders, and customers and is already shaping our future. With more than ten years of experience with utility energy-efficiency programs, initial results are promising, but many uncertainties remain.

Efforts to harness the utility sector to achieve greater energy efficiency have focused on three strategies:

◆ Demand-side management programs—utility-led efforts intended to affect the timing or amount of customer energy use. Examples include rebates, loans, energy audits, utility installation of efficient equipment, and load-management programs.

◆ Integrated resource planning—a technique used by utilities and regulators to develop flexible plans for providing reliable and economical electricity supply through a process that explicitly compares supply- and demand-side resource options on a consistent basis and usually has opportunities for public participation.

◆ Regulatory incentives for investment in energy-saving technologies adopted to offset the bias against energy-efficiency investments in traditional rate-making methods. Typically, utility profits have been based on the total value of capital invested and the amount of power sold—creating a strong financial disincentive against energy efficiency or other investments that could reduce power sales and utility revenues. Examples include mechanisms decoupling utility revenues from power sales, cost recovery or rate basing of efficiency programs expenditures, and performance bonuses and penalties.

More than thirty states have adopted integrated resource planning and demand-side management programs, and programs are being developed rapidly in most of the remaining states.

Reading Time: _____

Word Count: 560

Reading Speed: _____

Directions: Answer the following questions on the basis of the passage you just read. You may look back as often as necessary to find the correct answer. For each question, underline the answer you think is best.

1. It's plain that utilities have not helped their customers maximize savings because they
   - (A) have not invested in new technology
   - (B) are not willing to help customers
   - (C) are not aware of the new technologies available
   - (D) realize that power sources are already as efficient as they can be

2. According to this passage, what is the cause of the efficiency gap?
   - (A) technical problems
   - (B) potential savings
   - (C) consumers' disinterest
   - (D) at least four different reasons

3. Energy-efficiency programs can realize savings for
   - (A) consumers
   - (B) utilities
   - (C) shareholders
   - (D) all of the above

4. Among the risks the author cites for relying on greater energy efficiency are
   - (A) consumer distrust of new technologies
   - (B) concerns about equal distribution of profits
   - (C) fears that the savings will not be real
   - (D) problems with the utility sector itself

5. What is the relationship of electricity consumption to overall energy use?
   - (A) They are growing at the same rate.
   - (B) Electricity consumption is growing more quickly.
   - (C) Electricity consumption is growing more slowly.
   - (D) There is no relationship at all.

6. How many more megawatts of power does the author estimate will be needed?
   - (A) 1000
   - (B) 50,000 to 220,000
   - (C) 5000 to 22,000
   - (D) in excess of 500,000

7. Who will pay for this new construction?
(A) utility companies
(B) the federal government
(C) utility users
(D) the state government

8. According to the article, more and more people are coming to believe that
(A) new power plants are the wave of the future
(B) the federal government should step in and regulate the energy industry
(C) we should conserve energy rather than erect new power plants
(D) energy efficiency is an unworkable plan

9. Which of the following programs is the most popular?
(A) regulatory incentives
(B) integrated resource planning and demand-side management programs
(C) integrated resource planning and regulatory incentives
(D) demand-side management programs and regulatory incentives

10. This passage was most likely written by
(A) the speaker for a utility company
(B) a company bidding on a new power plant
(C) a disgruntled rate payer
(D) an unbiased observer

Answers

| 1. (A) | 3. (D) | 5. (B) | 7. (C) | 9. (B) |
| 2. (D) | 4. (C) | 6. (C) | 8. (A) | 10. (D) |

Reading Scores

Excellent readers	9–10 correct
Above-average readers	7–8 correct
Average readers	5–6 correct
Below-average readers	less than 4 correct

Conditions of Confinement

There are two areas—education and treatment—in which conformance to assessment criteria is generally high but in which we have no foundation for assessing the adequacy of services provided. Although there is extensive anecdotal and experiential evidence on the educational deficiencies and the emotional and mental health problems of juvenile offenders, we have no systematic empirical data on confined youths' educational or treatment needs and problems. Thus, we cannot determine whether facilities provide appropriate programs or whether juveniles make progress during confinement. Major new initiatives are needed to periodically collect such data.

Most juveniles are confined in facilities that have passed recent state or local fire, safety, and sanitation inspections. Despite that, during site visits we observed a large number of facilities at which fire exits were not marked or fire escape routes were not posted in living units, and a few at which fire exits were blocked with furniture or other objects.

We recommend that state and local fire codes for juvenile facilities be toughened and enforced more vigorously. In particular, we recommend that facilities be inspected more frequently, and that available enforcement authority be exercised more vigorously to correct violations. We also recommend that laws or regulations governing fire and life safety in juvenile facilities be as rigorous as those that apply to schools, hospitals, and other buildings.

We estimate, on average, confined juveniles are held in facilities that are 58 miles from where they live. (That distance varies by facility type, so that training schools are, on average, farther from juveniles' homes than are detention centers.) Distance and location (e.g., wilderness-based programs) affect juveniles' access to the community. Most confined juveniles have adequate opportunity to visit with families or attorneys, to contact volunteers, and to communicate by mail. However, telephone calls are an exception: Almost all juveniles can place a limited number of telephone calls per week, but 45 percent of confined juveniles are in facilities that do not permit them to receive telephone calls.

There is generally high conformance to most criteria that limit staff discretion. However, search authorization is an exception: Most confined juveniles are in facilities where line staff can authorize room searches and frisks. A substantial minority are in facilities where line staff can authorize strip searches. There was substantial variation in rates of searching, isolation, and restraint use among facilities. Relatively little of that variation could be explained by our analyses.

We recommend that more extensive comparison of conditions in facilities with high and low rates of use of search, isolation, and restraints be conducted in order to identify and test the rationales and effects of these variations in practice.

There are three areas in which conditions of confinement appear to be adequate: food, clothing, and hygiene; recreation; and living accommodations. With respect to the latter, conditions are somewhat more problematic. Detention centers generally have the least normalized and most institutionalized environments (sleeping rooms are starkly furnished, most residents wear uniforms, etc.). Nearly one third of all detained juveniles sleep in rooms that do not have natural light.

Reading Time: _____

Word Count: 470

Reading Speed: _____

Directions: Answer the following questions on the basis of the passage you just read. You may look back as often as necessary to find the correct answer. For each question, underline the answer you think is best.

1. Which of the following would make the best title for the first paragraph?
   (A) "Areas with Less Substantial Deficiencies"
   (B) "How to Improve Our Juvenile Services"
   (C) "Areas That Do Not Require Additional Funding"
   (D) "Education and Treatment Services"

2. The authors say that they cannot draw conclusions about educational services because
    (A) the area is so deficient that they do not know where to begin
    (B) there is too much anecdotal evidence
    (C) they do not have the facts they need
    (D) the offenders have severe emotional problems

3. Based on the information in the first paragraph, which of the following recommendations would the authors most likely make?
    (A) a study to document the educational needs of confined juvenile offenders
    (B) a study of juvenile offenders' emotional and mental health
    (C) a greater emphasis on safety
    (D) longer sentences for all juvenile offenders

4. To whom is this report most likely directed?
    (A) the parents or guardians of the incarcerated offenders
    (B) a state or governmental agency
    (C) scholars of the juvenile system
    (D) the court system

5. Most juvenile facilities are the same in all services *except*
    (A) access to attorneys
    (B) choice of facility
    (C) telephone privileges
    (D) ability to deal with volunteers

6. What is the most likely conclusion to paragraph 4?
    (A) All incarcerated juveniles be able to receive as well as make telephone calls.
    (B) All incarcerated juveniles be able to make as well as receive telephone calls.
    (C) No incarcerated juveniles have telephone privileges.
    (D) Incarcerated juveniles should not have as much access to families and attorneys.

7. That the majority of the staff conforms to the rules about discretion suggests that the
    (A) staff are poorly trained
    (B) rules are unfair
    (C) prisoners are well behaved
    (D) staff is skilled and caring

8. There is a substantial variation in rates of
   (A) searching, isolation, and restraint use
   (B) offender compliance with the staff and rules
   (C) visitation
   (D) escape attempts

9. Which of the areas mentioned in the final paragraph need the most improvement?
   (A) food
   (B) apparel
   (C) rooms
   (D) athletics

10. You can infer from this passage that the inspectors
   (A) were basically pleased with what they saw in their inspections of the juvenile facilities
   (B) did not know a great deal about juvenile facilities before their inspections and were shocked by what they saw
   (C) were paid by the parents of the incarcerated juveniles
   (D) found the juvenile facilities lacking in a substantial number of serious ways

Answers

| 1. (D) | 3. (A) | 5. (C) | 7. (D) | 9. (C) |
| 2. (C) | 4. (B) | 6. (A) | 8. (A) | 10. (D) |

Reading Scores

Excellent readers	9–10 correct
Above-average readers	7–8 correct
Average readers	5–6 correct
Below-average readers	less than 4 correct

Part 2

Developing Your Reading Abilities

Power Reading Facts

Experts estimate that an astonishing 80 to 90 percent of the information we need comes from what we read.

Increasingly, survival in the modern world demands new approaches to reading. You must be able to sift what is important from what is not to pick only the most crucial documents to read. Second, you must be able to integrate information with greater speed and skill by reading faster. Consider this, at 250 words per minute the average person needs one whole day to read a 300-page book. Power readers, reading at the rate of 750 words per minute, can finish that same book in less than three hours!

Power readers accomplish three times as much with their time!

Whether you are a professional working full time, returning student, homemaker, or someone looking to position yourself for the future, you can teach yourself to read faster. Here's how!

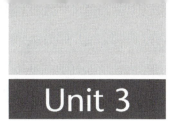

Unit 3

Techniques for Success

This will never be a civilized country until we expend more money for books than we do for chewing gum.

—Elbert Hubbard

The first step in becoming a power reader is to assemble the tools you need for success. The first and most important tool is your attitude. Think success. You *can* read more efficiently—if you want to. You *can* maximize your time and increase your efficiency. You *can* position yourself for the future.

Create a positive mindset. This will help you tap your potential and absorb information faster and more efficiently.

There are other important steps to take as well. Each can help you concentrate more fully. Before you go any further, read through this list. Try to follow each suggestion. You'll find the results well worth it!

Set Up a Reading Area

Human beings are remarkably adaptable creatures. We can function under the harshest conditions—but we function much better in an optimal setting. You can read on a moving train, in a dimly lit bus, in a noisy waiting room, or in a quiet park. But you will find that you will read better—faster, easier, and more efficiently—if you are reading in a suitable environment. Set aside a specific place as your reading area, and make it as pleasant as you can.

Establishing a set area for reading helps you concentrate. It's like priming the pump; once you sit down in your reading area, you'll be set to read faster and more easily than in other places. Making the area as pleasant as possible helps you associate reading with other pleasurable activities.

Reading from Video Display Terminals

The application of computer technology and the accompanying use of video display terminals (VDTs) are revolutionizing the American workplace and the way people read. In 1976, there were fewer than 700,000 VDTs in American offices; by 1986, there were nearly 30 million, and by even the most conservative estimates, there should be about *80 million VDTs* in the American workplace by the year 2000. If you are reading from a VDT, be sure that you have a comfortable work station, free from clutter, noise, and other distractions.

Select the Correct Chair

People often say to me, "Every time I read in bed, I fall asleep. What should I do?" The answer depends on your purpose. If you want to go to sleep, by all means read in bed. But if you want to get some reading done, you're much better off sitting in a chair! Select a comfortable chair that helps you sit in an upright position. If you are sitting up straight, you are less likely to lose concentration

If you are reading from a VDT, select a chair that provides the correct posture support for your back, arms, legs, and feet. Proper chair height and support to the lower region of the back are critical factors in reducing reading fatigue.

Hold the Reading Material Properly

Position the book so that the print at the top of the page will be the same distance from your eyes as the print at the bottom of the page. Hold the book a comfortable distance from your eyes, about 14 inches on the average. If you are reading from a VDT, make sure that you can see the screen without straining your neck, back, or arms.

Get a Good Light Source

Reading in poor light increases your chances of suffering from eyestrain. When you read in insufficient or excess light, you will be more apt to throw down the book or walk away from your computer. Read in natural light or under good artificial light. Avoid the kind of light that creates glare or focuses on the page only, leaving the rest of the room in darkness. Set up the lamp or light source so that the light is diffused. Use this simple test: If your eyes feel strained, readjust the light source.

Visual problems such as eyestrain and eye irritation are among the most frequently cited complaints of VDT users. When you read from a VDT, direct the light so that it does not shine in your eyes as you face the screen. In addition, make sure the lighting is adequate for you to see the text on the screen, but not so bright as to cause glare or discomfort. High illumination washes out the words on the display screen; therefore, illumination levels should be lower than those normally recommended for use with printed material. To prevent the visual discomfort caused by alternating light and dark areas, the difference in illumination between the VDT display screen, the horizontal work surface, and the surrounding areas should be minimized. Work station lighting should be easily adjustable and directed at source documents rather than at the display screen surface. You can also reduce eyestrain by taking vision breaks, which include looking up from the screen and staring at distant objects.

Keep It Cool

Try to keep the temperature around 65 degrees Fahrenheit. If the room is much warmer, you are apt to become sleepy; if it is cooler, you are likely to be uncomfortable and thus distracted. If 65 degrees feels cool to you, put on a sweater!

Check Your Eyes

Have your eyes checked annually. Always have your eye glasses fitted by a professional optometrist or ophthalmologist. Do not buy over-the-counter reading glasses. If you need glasses or contact lenses to read, be sure to wear them.

Get Sufficient Rest

During sleep, the body and brain rest, repair, and renew. Scientists know that just two nights without adequate sleep results in lower reading speed and comprehension. To maximize your reading speed and comprehension, be sure to get sufficient rest. Don't read if you are exhausted.

The fast pace of the Information Age demands full mental concentration. Give yourself every edge that you can!

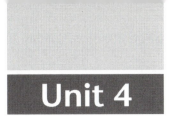

Unit 4

Skimming to Increase Speed

Some books are to be tasted, others to be swallowed, and some to be chewed and digested....

—*Francis Bacon*

Imagine that you are due in a meeting in 15 minutes, but have not read the 10,000-word report that will be discussed. What can you do? Or consider this scenario: You are trying to decide where to hold a one-day business retreat. You don't have the time to read through dozens of brochures or travel guides. What you need is a general idea of suitable and available accommodations. Is this possible? Because these and similar scenarios are commonplace today, it is imperative that you learn to read more quickly. One way to do this is through skimming.

Skimming is a very rapid method of reading that allows you to glance at a passage to find specific information. This method is especially useful when there is only one item of information that you want from a particular passage. With practice, you should be able to skim a page in five minutes—or less. Here are two methods for power skimming:

Power Reading Strategies

Method 1: Straight down the middle

- ◆ Run your eye down the middle of the page.

- ◆ Zero in on the facts you need.

Method 2: Crisscross

- ◆ First scan from the top left corner to the bottom right corner.

- ◆ Then scan from the top right corner to the bottom left corner.

Skim the following article to find the answers to these questions:

1. Where are the really interesting advances going to be made?

2. Why are huge databases useless?

3. What is the name of the Dow Jones News/Retrieval Service database retrieval service?

4. Why are these services important?

5. Who will be using such software in the future?

 ## A Software Revolution

The really interesting advances are going to be in software development. Computers haven't made our lives simpler. In fact, they have made reality more complicated. These things that were supposed to help us generate a whole lot of information actually generated a whole lot of data that has to be dealt with on a daily basis. Our customers have huge databases that they feel are the company's assets, but often there are so much data that they are virtually useless. Every single corporation is in that bind—or will be very shortly. They know that they have information about their clients, their suppliers, and their competitors, but they do not have a way to gather the data that can make it useful.

Dow Jones News/Retrieval Service has the DowQuest service. Here's how it works. Say that you have an article you like. You can ask for more similar articles. That's an example of something that is terribly complicated that doesn't seem very complicated to people not familiar with how computers operate. It's a primitive version of what some leading-edge computer companies are already doing: making software that provides a simple way of looking at huge amounts of data. It is going to change the way that business operates.

The software will do what a very fast, very skilled, and very dedicated librarian could do. You can ask the computer a question in everyday language and the software will sift through your corporate database, find all the pertinent information, and throw out what is not useful. What will this accomplish? Fewer, not more, things will come across your desk. And you will get what you need.

Up until now, it has been the scientists who have been using the supercomputer. In the future, you will see more business applications. For example, you might see an airline company using the software to decide how much to charge for a seat or how many seats to allocate to each fare class; a petrochemical company deciding how much of each product to manufacture given the kind of oil they have coming and the price they are paying for it. Business will make all these decisions more efficiently, thanks to the supercomputer and new software applications.

Reading Time: _____

Word Count: 330

Reading Speed: _____

Answers

1. They will be in software development.

2. Their information cannot be easily accessed.

3. It is called DowQuest.

4. They will screen the information flooding in and you will get what you need.

5. Businesses will be using it.

Power Skimming!

Imagine that you have read that all-important report but you're a little rusty on the details. You don't have the time to reread the entire report in depth, but you've got to be sure to remember the details. Perhaps a coworker has given you a book in your field. While you appreciate the gesture, you want to make sure that the book is worth your time before you spend a few hours reading it. You can't just skim—what if the coworker asks you some detailed questions? In these instances, and others like them, the answer is power skimming.

This method is ideal when you want to get a little more information than skimming provides, but still do not have time to read word for word. It is also an ideal method for reading technical articles, which are often more difficult to read than fiction, newspapers, and magazines. In these instances, take skimming one step further to power skimming. Follow these steps:

Power Reading Strategies

◆ Skim the text.

◆ Read through at your fastest rate.

◆ Underline important passages.

◆ Reread only the underlined passages.

Power skim the following article to find the answers to these questions.

1. By how much did the Consumer Price Index rise between February and March?

2. What were the three primary causes of this increase?

3. What amount of money in 1994 equaled the purchasing power that $10 bought in 1982–1983?

4. Is the report data adjusted for changes in seasonal purchasing?

5. What states are included in this consumer price region?

 Bureau of Labor Statistics Report

The Consumer Price Index for New York–northeastern New Jersey rose 0.3 percent between February and March, the Regional Commissioner of Labor Statistics reported this week. The commissioner attributed the bulk of the March rise to increases in apparel, typically up at this time of the year, as well as household furnishings and operations, and homeowners' costs. These increases were partially offset by declines for transportation, grocery store foods, and other renters' costs, such as lodging away from home. For the year ending March 1994, consumer prices in the area increased 2.5 percent, in line with last month's rate but below the 3.4 percent annual increase for the same month a year ago.

With the New York–northeastern New Jersey Consumer Price Index for all Urban Consumers at 157.9 in March (1982–84 = 100),

$15.79 was required to purchase what $10 could in the 1982–84 base period. The purchasing power of the dollar was 63.3 cents in 1982–84 dollars and 21.9 cents in 1967 dollars.

The Consumer Price Index for Urban Wage Earners and Clerical Workers was also up 0.3 percent in March.

Data in this analysis are not seasonally adjusted. As a result, month-to-month changes may reflect the impact of seasonal influences. The New York–northeastern New Jersey area comprises the five boroughs of New York City; Nassau, Suffolk, Westchester, Rockland, Putnam, and Orange counties in New York State; Bergen, Essex, Hudson, Hunterdon, Middlesex, Monmouth, Morris, Ocean, Passaic, Somerset, Sussex, and Union counties in New Jersey; and Fairfield County and parts of Lichfield and New Haven counties in Connecticut.

Reading Time: _____

Word Count: 250

Reading Speed: _____

Answers

1. It rose 0.3 percent.

2. The increase was due to a rise in sales of apparel, household furnishings and operations, and homeowners' costs.

3. You would need $15.79.

4. No, it is not.

5. New York, New Jersey, and Connecticut are included.

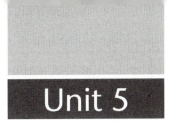

Unit 5

Increasing Your Span of Perception

These are not books, lumps of lifeless paper, but minds alive on the shelves. From each of them goes out its own voice...and just as the touch of a button on our set will fill the room with music, so by taking down one of these volumes and opening it, one can call into range the voices of a man far distant in time and space, and hear him speaking to us, mind to mind, heart to heart.

—Gilbert Highet

Why don't people make the most of their reading ability? There are a number of reasons, including regression, subvocalization, lack of training, and reading word for word. Looking at each reason more closely will help you become a power reader.

Regression

The first reason why many people read far more slowly than they could is because they backtrack to read over specific words, phrases, or sentences. Going back to reread is called regression. Reading slows down even more because at the end of each line, the eye zeroes in on the last word, creating what is called a fixation. In most cases, the process is not even deliberate; most regression takes place because the reader has been distracted from the page. Feeling insecure, the reader returns to the passage and rereads it, losing precious time. In actuality, regression does not improve comprehension—it actually reduces it. Why? Because going back over the same words and phrases causes the reader to lose track of the sense of the entire passage, which further undermines comprehension. This causes great frustration, further reducing speed.

Subvocalization

Another reason why people don't maximize their reading potential is because they silently read to themselves. Called subvocalization, this undesirable habit slows your reading down like a rush-hour traffic jam on the expressway. As we read, we are able to grasp groups of words at a time, entire phrases and even sentences. When we subvocalize, we drastically reduce the number of words we read at a time. Here's proof:

average speaking rate	=	150 words per minute
average reading rate	=	250 words per minute

Clearly, if we speak each word silently to ourselves, we're losing 100 words per minute!

Lack of Training

For most people, formal reading education stops in school—usually in grade school. As a result, even the best educated people may be reading at the same rate they learned in elementary school. For years, they have compensated by simply reading for longer and longer hours. We know that simply will not be possible in the future: There will be too much to read and too little time in which to accomplish it.

Reading Word for Word

Most of us learned to read by looking at each letter in turn and sounding it out. For instance, if you saw the word *hat*, you would have said "huh-ah-t, makes hat." After you figured out the word's sound, you could grasp its meaning. To see what we mean, read this sentence letter by letter:

National parks are the greatest idea we ever had: They reflect America at its best.

Your reading picked up speed when you were able to put the words together to create sentences, usually around the first or second grade. Unfortunately, many readers remain fixed at this stage. They read every word—which dramatically reduces their speed and comprehension.

What Is Perception Span?

Your perception span is the number of letters or symbols your eye can perceive and understand in a single sweep. The greater your span of perception, the more you can read at a single glance. Increase your span of perception, and your reading speed will soar.

The average reader has a perception span of twenty-four letters or symbols, usually about four words. With practice, this span can be doubled and even tripled. What's your perception span? Take this easy self-test to find out.

Test Your Perception Span

Read the following three passages to see which is most comfortable for your field of vision. Read at your usual pace. Then arrange the passages from easiest to most difficult. Determine your current span of perception from the easiest passage. Count the number of letters in the passage.

Passage 1

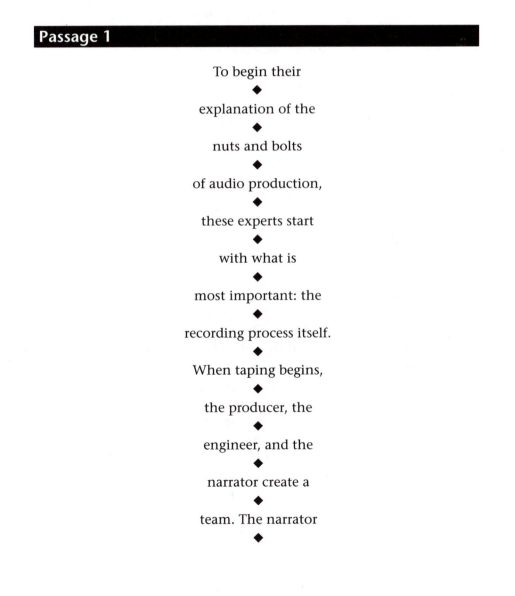

To begin their
◆
explanation of the
◆
nuts and bolts
◆
of audio production,
◆
these experts start
◆
with what is
◆
most important: the
◆
recording process itself.
◆
When taping begins,
◆
the producer, the
◆
engineer, and the
◆
narrator create a
◆
team. The narrator
◆

sits at a table

◆

with a lamp,

◆

a pitcher of

◆

water, and a

◆

glass. The narrator

◆

begins reading into

◆

a microphone that

◆

is shielded with

◆

a circular windscreen

◆

to cut down on

◆

exhaled air. The

◆

producer and the

◆

engineer sit behind

◆

a recording console

◆

in the control

◆

room and run

◆

the tape recorder.

◆

The quality of

◆

the digital audiotape

◆

is crucial.

◆ ◆ ◆ ◆

Passage 2

During recording sessions, the
◆
producer directs the narrator
◆
on his or her interpretation
◆
of the text. In essence,
◆
the producer establishes the
◆
tone of the production.
◆
The engineer's task
◆
is to edit the tape
◆
as it is being recorded,
◆
much as an editor revises
◆
the text of a printed book.
◆
The engineer listens for the
◆
sounds of pages being turned,
◆
low breathing, and mispronounced words.
◆
The tape can be stopped
◆
at any time. If the editing
◆
is not squeaky clean,
◆
the total effect of the reading
◆
may be spoiled.
◆ ◆ ◆ ◆

Passage 3

The first challenge is selecting the best possible
◆
narrator. There are various possibilities. Many
◆
producers prefer to work with professionals. They
◆
can consider tapes that pour in every day from
◆
unsolicited narrators, a source that seldom pays off.
◆
Or they can hire famous actors and actresses.
◆
These narrators can be difficult to work with because
◆
they are often not accustomed to sustained reading.
◆
Probably the best narrators are the professional
◆
voice-over actors in New York who record for a living.
◆
Many of them were trained on the old
◆
16-RPM masters, when making a mistake
◆
meant breaking the master and starting over.
◆
Now, with the high-tech excellence of
◆
digital recording, these experienced narrators can
◆
read for hours without seeming to take a breath.
◆
Many narrators work six hours a day, six days
◆
a week, to complete a project within schedule.
◆

My perception span is: _____

The following activities can help you increase your span of perception. We recommend that you complete them in the order stated.

Span Card

One of the quickest ways to increase your span of perception is through this visual aid. On a 3×5 index card, draw a rectangle 3 inches long and $^1/_2$ inch high. This rectangle should be $^1/_2$ inch down from the top of the card and $^1/_4$ inch in from the right side. Using a sharp pair of scissors or a razor, cut out the rectangle you have drawn.

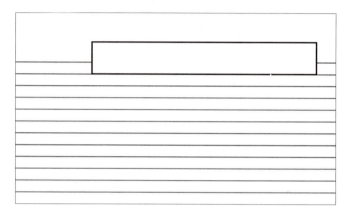

Hold the card in your left hand. Center the card down the middle of a passage. Move it down as you read. The card helps keep your eye focused on the page. As your span of perception increases, make new cards, each with a longer opening. The next card, for example, may have an opening 3 $^1/_4$ inches long, 3 $^1/_2$ inches long, and so on. Try the card on this passage:

All health care information systems, whether paper or computer, present confidentiality and privacy problems. Computerization can reduce some concerns about privacy in patient data and worsen others, but it also raises new problems. Computerization increases the quantity and availability of data and enhances the ability to link data, raising concerns about demands for new information beyond those for which it was originally collected. The potential for abuse by trusted insiders to a system is of particular concern.

In addition, special policy problems are raised by computerization. Proposed use of unique patient identifiers assigned at birth and retained through a patient's lifetime raises concerns among privacy advocates, who claim that if the Social Security number is used for this purpose, linkage

of a wide variety of information resulting in dossier-type files on indi-
viduals would be possible. Policies governing requirements for informed
consent could be challenged as well, since currently patients have limited
access to their health care record and may have little choice in consenting
to its disclosure for certain purposes.

Eye Focus 1

Focus your eyes just above the center of each line. Read the letters on
either side, without moving your eyes from the center of the page. Continue reading this way, as you move your eyes down the page. Move as
quickly as you can, spending no more than one second per line. Avoid
sounding out the letters to yourself. If you do find that you are
subvocalizing, stop, exhale, and count to three. Then continue reading.

G	GHT	P
K	LUY	M
M	YRE	B
Q	RET	X
A	SRE	H
J	JCS	Y
L	POL	A
V	TEP	F
K	TQO	R
G	OIU	Q
L	GEX	I
R	GCX	Y
P	LBH	R
Y	QER	H
C	RQO	J
K	TER	L
H	FRE	G
G	TZK	Q

Eye Focus 2

Now try the same exercise with words. When you read one word, you
focus directly on it, like this:

technology

When you encounter two words together, focus on a spot in the middle of them. Try it with these two words:

technology ◆ explosion

The same process holds true for three words: keep your eye trained on the middle:

current technology explosion

The more words you can grasp in a single sweep, the greater your span of perception. This, in turn, speeds up your reading and comprehension rates.

As you complete this exercise, keep your eye focused on the middle of the page. Remember not to shift your eyes back and forth and to keep your attention focused on the center word. Try to take in larger groups of information as you read on.

The	National	Park
Service	was	founded
by	Congress	in
1916	to	conserve
park	resources	and
to	provide	for
their	use	"by
the	public	so
as	to	leave
them	unimpaired	for
the	enjoyment	of
future	generations."	In
1967	Congress	moved
to	create	a
private	National	Park
Foundation	to	actively
seek	additional	funds
for	the	parks
from	people	and
corporations	all	over.

Eye Focus 3

As you have very likely discovered by this point, it is easier to take in large groups of words when they make sense. Compare these two groups of words:

from one care facility to

As a result of the linkage of computers,

The second group is three words longer, yet it is easier to grasp in a single eye sweep. Why? Because the words make sense and function as a single unit of thought. As you widen your span of perception, try to seize and process groups of words that express a complete idea. Try this exercise to see what we mean. Remember to keep your eye in the middle of the word group as you scan down the page.

The medical record is the primary source

◆

for much of the health care information

◆

sought by parties outside the

◆

direct health care delivery relationship.

◆

These data are important because

◆

health care information can influence

◆

decisions about an individual's access to credit,

◆

admission to educational institutions,

◆

and ability to secure employment

◆

and to obtain insurance.

◆

Inaccuracies in the information,

◆

or its improper disclosure,

can deny an individual access to

◆

these basic necessities of life and

◆

can threaten an individual's personal

◆

and financial well-being.

◆

At the same time,

◆

accurate and comprehensive health care information

◆

is critical to the quality of health care delivery

◆

and to the doctor-patient relationship.

◆

Many believe that the efficacy of

◆

the health care relationship

◆

depends on the patient understanding that

◆

the information recorded by a physician

◆

will not be disclosed.

◆

Without these assurances,

◆

many patients might refuse

◆

to provide physicians with

◆

certain types of information needed

◆

to render appropriate care.

◆ ◆ ◆ ◆

Now combine all the power reading techniques you have learned in these lessons. As you read this passage, keep your eye trained on the middle of each line, and try to take in the largest possible number of words with each sweep of your eye. We've arranged the word groups to help guide your eye. Note the time and begin reading.

Support for Mentally Ill Offenders in the Community: Milwaukee's Community Support Program

Summary

Every day our crowded, overburdened jails and probation departments face

yet another challenge—dealing with offenders who are mentally ill

and require medication, close monitoring, and other services.

Many of these persons have been in and out of jails and hospitals.

Few have homes or jobs, and more and more of them are drug-addicted as

well. Their own untreated, often psychotic, behavior may have been the

cause of their being arrested in the first place.

Milwaukee faced up to the problem fifteen years ago

when it developed a program to keep these offenders out of jail,

out of the hospital, and under close community supervision.

The Community Support Program, run by a private nonprofit agency,

provided an alternative to incarceration for this

population through a mix of coercion,

incentives, housing assistance, money management,

and therapeutic support services.

The program does this for $3,000 a year per client—

less than it would cost for intensive outpatient treatment

in local mental health systems. This Program Focus describes how the

program works and how it gained community acceptance.

It is an approach that offers a ray of hope to cities seeking a just, humane,

and realistic means of dealing with mentally ill offenders while protecting

the wider community as well.

Key Elements

The program was developed in 1978,

when WCS noticed the growing

numbers of chronically mentally ill persons

coming into Milwaukee's courts and jails. Since then,

the county has copied the basic design and funded

three other community support programs,

two under contract with private organizations and

a third operated directly by county officials.

The program model includes the following five defining elements,

all of which can be adapted quite easily to other jurisdictions.

These include:

◆ Medical and Therapeutic Services

Medication is prescribed, administered five days a week, and closely monitored by a pharmacy on the premises. Psychotherapy and group sessions are also available, and case management services are provided to all clients to help them obtain primary health care.

◆ Money Management

The program arranges to be the legal recipient for the client's Social Security and other disability benefits. The client's fixed expenses (rent, for example) are paid directly by the program. The remainder is given to the client on a daily basis—after the client has taken his or her prescribed medication.

◆ Housing and Other Support Services

Intensive casework is undertaken to provide for the client's basic needs, either after arrest or upon release from jail or a hospital. This includes referral to other social service agencies, if needed. Housing in the community is arranged directly by the program, and daily living is monitored by periodic home visits.

◆ Day Reporting and Close Monitoring

Most clients are required to report to the clinic daily, where they can either stay for a brief period to take their medications and get their money for longer periods. The daily observation and interaction with the clients enables the staff to monitor behavior and to spot

Introduction

Persons suffering chronic mental illnesses are
frequently caught up in the criminal justice system,
but justice agencies are usually ill equipped to
respond effectively to the problems they pose.
Jailing them keeps them off the streets,
but this provides only a short-term solution at a high price.
Probation may be warranted in some cases,
but conventional supervision and services are often insufficient.
Many mentally ill persons need the most elementary of necessities,
as well as medication, and they require more intensive monitoring than
most probation departments are able to devote to them.

"Carrot and Stick" Approach

The Wisconsin Correctional Service (WCS),
a private not-for-profit organization in Milwaukee,
has established an innovative Community Support Program (CSP)
that adopts a "carrot and stick" approach to managing mentally ill
offenders in the community, most of whom are schizophrenic.
Since many of the program's clients come to the attention of the criminal
justice agencies, formal legal authority is used initially
to get offenders into the program.
The program is also well suited to serving mentally ill persons who
have not yet come into the criminal justice system but may be at risk of
doing so. Many WCS clients have run afoul of the law because
they are actively psychotic and not medicated,
and with the court's authority most can be convinced
to accept medications. Once engaged in the program,
many offenders comply willingly with its requirements
because they receive substantial benefits, various social services,
and life supports. Indeed, some choose to stay in the program for years,
well beyond the cessation of their legal obligations.

when changes in medication are needed. Failure to report is noted, and clients are located.

◆ Participation

Although clients must agree to enter the treatment program, their choice is constrained by other less desirable alternatives, including jail. Because many mentally ill persons are difficult to manage and resist being medicated, the combination of supportive services backed by firm legal authority is effective in bringing them into treatment. Program administrators believe what keeps clients in the program are the benefits. Prior to coming into the program, many of the clients are homeless and without any means of support. By helping them get shelter, income, and medication, the program creates a powerful incentive for staying.

Program Operations

The program operates out of a small clinic located
in a residential neighborhood. The clinic has a friendly, relaxed feeling
about it, without the trappings of a more institutional setting.
Clients even have a room where they can socialize with
each other or just relax during the daytime.
Clinic staff are readily available to all clients
and offer a broad range of services.
Three full-time nurses provide clinical support to clients, who, in
addition to psychological distress, often need primary health care
evaluation and referral to medical services.
A part-time psychiatrist diagnoses clients and prescribes them
psychotropic medications as needed. The pharmacy staff dispenses
all medications and manages the required record keeping.
Four full-time case managers have a caseload of sixty clients each.
Several staff service members help clients obtain government benefits
and manage their money. Daily allowances are given out by a cashier.
Two staff persons work to obtain housing for those who need it and to
help manage clients' ongoing relationships with their landlords.
A small management and administrative staff direct overall operations.
The program has the capacity to serve 250 clients at any one time.

Entry into the Program

Clients come to the CSP through various routes. Some are identified by workers in other programs that WCS operates for Milwaukee's municipal courts. Others are referred by probation and parole officers or by private attorneys. A small percentage come into the program on their own. Some are referred by psychiatric hospitals.

Clients

The typical CSP client is a male in his mid-thirties who has never been married, has some secondary education, and has a diagnosed major mental illness. The majority had at least two prior arrests on their record. Clients entering the program in 1992 averaged 75 days in psychiatric hospitals during the past two years.

Although the number of admitted persons has remained constant over the past several years, the clinical conditions of the clients have changed. There has been an upsurge of drug users, who have more serious histories of institutionalization and demonstrate more frequent relapses.

Many clients have a history of noncompliance with outpatient treatment programs.

Success Factors

The program's primary objectives are to keep persons afflicted with chronic mental illnesses out of the local jails and hospitals and to help them live independently. Although the program has not been formally evaluated, it appears to be meeting all its goals. Indeed, county officials are so convinced of the program's success that they have dedicated scarce State and Federal aid dollars to fund three other similar programs.

By creating a system for identifying ill persons brought into court and jail and creating a programmatic alternative that the courts use, the program is undoubtedly reducing the number of mentally ill persons in jail. The program's administrators report that in recent years the proportion of jail inmates diagnosed as mentally ill has been small— about 3 percent—and that the proportion was much larger prior to the program's creation.

Perhaps the program's accomplishment is that it has devised
an important support service that did not previously exist in a fiscal
environment that has not encouraged public expenditures
for the poor and needy.

Reading Time: _____

Word Count: 1,370

Reading Speed: _____

Unit 6

Using Eye–Hand Reading

Power Reading Facts
President John F. Kennedy could read 1,200 words per minute; another president, Theodore Roosevelt, read an entire book every day before he ate breakfast.

How can you tune up your brain to master even greater blocks of type? How can you read fast enough to complete a book a day? One of the most effective ways to become a master reader is to teach your hands to help your eyes take in more words, more quickly. There is some controversy about eye–hand reading, but we have found that if this method is properly used, it can be one of the fastest ways to powerful reading. Why? Here are the top three reasons:

♦ Running your hand across the page helps you focus on important words, details, and ideas. This helps you key into the most crucial facts and ignore extraneous details.

♦ Tracing your hand down the page automatically leads your eye down the type. This helps you move forward, not backward, over the lines. You will have fewer regressions.

♦ Moving your hand down the page forces you to read faster than you can speak. As a result, you read at a visual, not a vocal, rate. This helps you eliminate subvocalizations.

One of the most impressive advantages of the eye–hand reading method is its versatility: There are three main methods, so you can select the one that suits your personal reading purpose and style. But try all the methods before you make your choice because you may decide to use more than one. For example, you may settle on one method for reading technical reports and memos, another for newspapers and magazines.

Each method requires you to move your hand across and down a line of type; the direction of the motion makes the difference. Start with a choice of instruments.

Make a Marker

A marker can help you follow a line of type. You can make your own marker by cutting a strip of paper 6 inches long and 1 inch wide. Use stiff cardboard so it holds up; select a neutral color such as white, buff, or tan so that you are not distracted.

Use a Pen or Pencil

Many people are comfortable with this method, which is handy to use when you are reading technical material, where you are likely to stop reading to take notes. Be sure to drag the wrong side—the eraser or pen cap—down the page or you will deface the text. Or, use an unsharpened pencil or a capped pen.

Use One Finger

Many people find the best marker is their left index finger, leaving the right hand free to turn the pages. This works especially well with right-handed people; lefties may want to try the reverse, using the index finger on their right hand and turning the pages with their left hand.

Use Two Fingers

Some people are more comfortable using their index and third fingers together. Experiment to find the one technique that works best for you.

Method 1: Single-line

This is the most commonly used eye–hand method because it's fast and easy. Even after they have learned more sophisticated methods, many people return to this technique when they are reading difficult technical material. Master the single-line method and you're well on your way to significant increases in reading speed and comprehension.

Start by selecting a marker. Let's assume that you are using the index finger on your left hand, but the choice is up to you. Place your reading material on a table or a desk. Make sure that you have plenty of room to swing your arm. Then it's only three easy steps to faster reading!

Power Reading Strategy

1. Place your finger on the first word of the first line of type and focus your eyes *slightly* in front of your fingers.

2. Move your finger from left to right across the line of type as you follow with your eyes.

3. When your eye reaches the right margin, move your finger slightly up and to the right to prevent fixations or abrupt stops.

Repeat the process, moving your finger down to the next line of type. To prevent fatigue, be sure to keep your head still and your elbow close to your body. Here's what it looks like:

Today the imperative for U.S. involvement in world events is

our role as world leaders and the chaotic conditions which prevail

and threaten global security. World disorder erupted when the

Soviet Union collapsed and the restraining forces of a bipolar world

were removed.

How well can you use the single-line method? Find out by taking this test. Check the time, read the passage without using a marker, and jot down your time. Then read a passage of similar content and length, using the single-line method. See which time is better.

America's New Challenge

Over the past fifty years, the United States has built the premier research and laboratory system in the world. Today, it numbers some seven hundred federal facilities, with an unparalleled network of scientists and engineers and a legacy of expertise and innovation....Now we must turn these vast resources to meet the next challenge—winning the global economic competition.
—Admiral James D. Watkins, U.S. Navy (Retired)

History is full of instances where technology has revolutionized energy supply sources and our effectiveness in putting them to human service. Americans in the 1980s, for example, demonstrated a remarkable ability to use advanced technologies to improve energy efficiency and save dollars. New insights about geology and new technologies for exploring and extracting energy resources have restocked our domestic energy reserves more than once.

Today's global economy is driven by technology. The pace at which today's technology flows from research to commercial product is astonishing. Our ability to meet the economic, environmental, and energy security challenges of the next century will depend on our ability to develop new technologies and open new markets where these technologies can be employed quickly and flexibly.

Meeting the New Challenge

Every sector in American society has a role to play in meeting this new challenge—industry, labor, academia, and government on all levels. Science and technology development, transferring technology to the marketplace, and developing scientists and engineers through education represent three high-priority areas playing major roles in virtually every aspect of this mission. Scientific and technology advances are critical to achieving the energy, economic, and environmental objectives of the National Energy Strategy—the most comprehensive energy strategy in U.S. history.

Recognizing technology's role in meeting America's new challenge, the National Technology Initiative was launched in 1992. The initiative, a multiagency effort, is aimed at promoting the U.S. industry's use of government-developed technology to strengthen our economy and compete overseas more effectively.

As the federal government's largest research and development (R&D) agency, the DOE has a particularly crucial role in stimulating creative inquiry, fostering invention, and commercializing innovation. DOE's vast research and design activities cover every aspect of energy production and use: fossil fuels, such as oil, natural gas, and coal; nuclear power, including such advanced forms as fusion energy; renewable energy, such as solar, wind, and geothermal power; and energy conservation and efficiency in buildings, industry, and transportation. DOE also conducts a large program of research in the basic sciences that bear on energy, such as physics, chemistry, the geosciences, the life sciences, and medical science.

Environmental restoration and waste management is DOE's fastest growing program area. We are developing advanced cleanup and waste minimization technologies that promise not only environmental progress in our country, but the opportunity to tap into huge markets around the world. DOE's technology transfer programs contribute to the successful commercialization of new products, helping solve industrial manufacturing problems, and helping state and local governments influence the rate at which new technologies and practices are accepted by industry and the general public.

What About the Future?
The twentieth century has been called "The American Century." Our extraordinary leadership in defeating monarchic imperialism in World War I, fascism in World War II, and communism in the Cold War, combined with the tremendous outpouring of our knowledge and wealth, justify that designation. Yet some observers, especially overseas, are predicting America's decline in the future.

Among tomorrow's challenges will be increasing the rate at which productive capacity of the U.S. economy grows. Productivity improves principally from the introduction of new technology. Technological innovations in agriculture, textiles, commerce, transportation, communication, health, defense, electronics, and energy have played famous roles in transforming society, creating jobs, and promoting economic growth.

Americans have a long history of shaping their own destiny and meeting challenges through technological progress. Developing and making full use of marketable technologies will be critical to sustaining the leadership the United States exercises in energy security, environmental quality, and economic prosperity.

Reading Time:_____

Method 2: Center Method
The center method focuses your eye on the middle of the page. Since you are reading far fewer words, you can read and absorb information much, much faster. In fact, many power readers find that the center method helps them read more than twice as fast as any other speed reading technique! First select a marker, such as your left index finger. Then follow these three key steps.

Power Reading Strategy
1. Place your finger under the first word in the middle of the page as you focus your eyes in front of your finger.
2. Move your finger from left to right across the line of type as you follow with your eyes.
3. When your finger reaches a few inches from the right margin, swing it to the middle of the next line.

As you pick up speed with this method, try to move in the margins on both sides. The closer your eye is to the middle, the less type you are processing. Remember this equation: fewer words = greater speed.

Don't use a spacebar to line up text. If you are used to working on a typewriter you might expect to use the spacebar to align individual lines. This technique works if you are using a monospaced font, such as Courier, in which every letter has the same width. However, you will probably want to use a more attractive proportionally spaced font, in which an *m* is wider than an *a*, for example. If you try to use the spacebar to line up proportionally spaced text, the text may not be aligned in the printed document.

Test your understanding of the center method by taking this test. Note your starting time. Read the passage, using your pacer to trace the middle of the passage. Then note your ending time and calculate your reading rate. See how it compares to your previous reading rates.

Changing Boundaries

An Interdependent World

Ideas, technologies, trade products, investments, communications, and people from many lands are moving across national boundaries with increasing ease and in growing numbers as the world becomes more interdependent. This trend is expected to continue and perhaps accelerate substantially in the 1990s and beyond, resulting in greater internationalization of the U.S. economy. This development offers unprecedented opportunities and challenges for our federal system and its ability to serve the American people. The United States government alone no longer can shield its state and local governments as it could in the past from adverse international forces that open state and local governments to a global economy that is increasingly competitive, interdependent, technological, interwoven, multicultural, multipolar, and subject to a multitude of influences from national governments, international organizations, transnational corporations, multinational public interest groups, and the federal and local governments of many nations. This rapid internationalization is requiring American state and local governments to revamp as well as develop their own export programs, cultural exchanges, tourist programs, immigrant services, and other policies toward foreign affairs in response to vital issues that confront them daily from abroad.

The Need for a Solid Infrastructure

If the U.S. economy is to be competitive with the economies of other nations, it needs to be based on an excellent physical infrastructure, reasonable taxation and regulation of businesses, a well qualified and highly adaptable workforce, flexible state-of-the art industries, and equal and open opportunities for all citizens to contribute to and benefit from prosperity. State and local governments have primary roles in each of these fields, and increasingly they are bringing such factors together into coherent economic development programs designed to attract and hold business forms, jobs, investments, and tourism, and to link economic growth more effectively to education and public well-being.

The Role of Private Enterprise

State and local governments by themselves, of course, do not hold all the keys to international competitiveness. Private enterprise is the foundation of America's economy, and it is the federal government that sets the overall policy framework within which the private sector and state and local governments can operate in the global arena. The federal government has vital responsibilities for macroeconomic policy making, affecting such matters as the cost of capital, the rates of capital formation, value of the dollar, and basic trade relationships. In addition, the federal government traditionally has played significant roles in antitrust regulation, basic scientific research, and foreign commerce in general. The federal government also has responsibility for immigration and refugee policies, which can have substantial effects on state and local budgets and services and on the ability to recruit needed talent.

The Key Ingredient

The key ingredient in competitiveness, however, is private sector entrepreneurship. Public policy—federal, state, and local—can encourage or discourage this activity, but seldom can it provide it directly. There is considerable controversy about the effects of current federal monetary policies on the entrepreneurial capacities of American business. Because these are matters of great importance to the U.S. competitive position, they need serious and continuing attention.

Reading Time:	_____
Word Count:	480
Reading Speed:	_____

Method 3: Double-line

The double-line method gives you much greater speed by helping you process even greater chunks of print. Use this method on less technical materials, like magazines and newspapers. Once again select a guiding instrument, such as your left index finger. Then follow these three key steps:

Power Reading Strategy

1. Place your finger under the first word; focus your eyes in front of your finger.

2. Move your finger from left to right across the line of type as you follow with your eyes.

3. When your eye reaches the right margin, skip down a line. Then repeat steps 1 and 2.

As you become more comfortable with this method, try to skip two lines in place of one. The more type you can bite off a line, the faster you will read. The double-line method looks like this:

Dave was indicted for murder, Bud as an accomplice. They were **moved nightly from jail to jail because of the intense feel**-ing against them throughout the country. Bud, the star witness, **implicated his brother fully. The jury reached a verdict** on the third ballot—guilty. Dave was sentenced to death; Bud, to **life imprisonment.**

◆ ◆ ◆ ◆

Take the following test to try your hand at the double-line method. Remember to skip a line or even two, if you can. Use your finger or marker to force your eye to move more quickly. Be sure to keep track of your time to see what effect this method has on your reading rate.

Spartans Facing Desperate Times

It was one of those torrid afternoons in the city that made you feel like you were locked in a steam machine. It was so hot and humid that a haze settled over the parking lot and made it difficult to see the empty spaces. Yet the Spartans were making the plays that would be the backbone of their 6–4 victory over the Rockets yesterday.

It was their defense and a 437-foot homer by Steven Borowicy that snapped a tie at 4 in the bottom of the seventh and swung the afternoon to the Spartans. The collision of bat and ball made the kind of sound only a true home-run hitter can detonate. Borowicy happens to be one of the best. The announcement that the ball remained airborne for 437 feet may have been Spartan propaganda, but it had to be close.

The ball didn't settle down until it landed in a small tree at the back of Ellsworth Park behind the Spartans' bullpen in deep left-centerfield. The Spartans added their fifth run that inning as James Wass singled, stole second and third, and came home on a sacrifice fly by Ric Taylor.

Sitting on the bench after the game, trying to breathe in the turgid air, Dennis O'Brien recalled two crucial plays by Robert Swantek. "All those years of hitting .350, .360," O'Brien said. "Everybody knows that Swantek is a power hitter, and man, can he make big plays."

The twenty-eight-year-old second baseman isn't known for his range, but he does have a sharp awareness of where he is and what he can do on a playing field. These skills have served the Spartans well. Swantek dived to his left, did a full turn along the ground, and came up throwing quickly and accurately to cut down Sam Fitzpatrick cold. Swanket made another spectacular diving play on a bunt in the eighth to get Luis Jackson.

The sixth was a difficult inning for Hernando Perez, but it was even more difficult for Fitzgerald, who finally figured out the way not to get thrown out at first as he whacked a line drive off the right-field fence. His problem came when he tried to stretch the hit into a double. Swantek threw a strike to Mike Kessman, who put the tag on the sliding Fitzgerald.

"The ball beat me to the wall," said a dripping Swantek. "Next thing you try to do is to get in a good position for a throw. I know I was sweating so much that I threw Kessman a real sinker." The Spartans had gained a valuable out in an inning in which a tiring Perez would go on to strand two base runners. Perez has had continued problems with his hip, which had stiffened up noticeably since the bottom of the fifth.

If not for another injury to Brett Ellis—a cramped hamstring that is not considered serious—the Spartans would have had an unqualified good night, complete with solid relief work by winning pitcher Bob Harris, and even an RBI for wallflower Tim Begar. Unexpected indeed.

Reading Time:	_____
Word Count:	400
Reading Speed:	_____

Focusing on Words

When we read too fast or too slowly, we understand nothing.
—Blaise Pascal

Average readers waste an astonishing one-quarter of their reading time looking at empty space, not words. You can pick up your reading speed and comprehension by learning to focus on the words, not on the spaces around them. Here's how.

Untrained readers tend to focus on the first word of the first line and follow that line to the end. What happens? Half the readers' span of perception is wasted in the margin! In Unit 5, you learned how to increase your perception span through different techniques. Power readers read faster and better by starting the reading process several words into the line rather than at the left margin. Extend this thinking: It makes sense to stop reading not at the last word, but rather several words before the end of the line. Follow these steps:

Power Reading Strategy

◆ Start reading two or three words into the line of type—about one inch in from the margin.

◆ Stop reading two or three words before the end of the line of type—about one inch in from the margin.

◆ Focus on the words, not the margin.

◆ Don't skip words.

◆ Continue this process, gradually beginning and ending your reading further and further from the margin. To adjust your focus, set your span of perception an inch or more in from the margin.

Try this technique on the following passage. To help you, we've drawn focus lines down each side of the page. Be sure to keep track of your time as you read so you can calculate your reading speed.

Osteoarthritis:
Humanity's Oldest Disease

Osteoarthritis is one of the world's oldest diseases. Skeletons of dinosaurs that lived 50 to 70 million years ago show abundant evidence of osteoarthritis. Signs of it have also been found in the bones of cavemen and Egyptian mummies.

Osteoarthritis occurs when the cartilage and other tissues that make a joint work properly begin to break down. As the smooth cartilage that protects the surface of the joints begins to wear away, the ends of the bones become unprotected. Without their normal gliding surface, joints become more painful and difficult to move.

Familiar to most people because it is the most common kind of arthritis, osteoarthritis affects more than 17 million Americans. Throughout history, almost every walking animal has been susceptible to this painful joint disease.

Osteoarthritis was at one time considered the inevitable result of normal wear and tear on the joints during a person's lifetime. It is much more common in people over forty, and almost everyone over sixty has it to some degree. However, researchers now think there are probably several factors leading to osteoarthritis. It can develop from overuse or abuse of a joint, such as from an injury, from being overweight, from an inborn abnormality in the joint itself, or from repeated use.

Cave dwellers who had osteoarthritis probably knew very little about how to control the pain and deformity, and so could do little to help themselves. Things are different today. Although there is still no cure for the condition, today's physicians know a great deal about alleviating much of the pain of osteoarthritis. The condition can usually be effectively treated with combinations of medication, rest, exercise, and sometimes surgery prescribed by a physician.

Early symptoms of osteoarthritis are usually stiffness and pain in certain joints such as the fingers, hips, knees, and spine. If you have these warning signs, contact your physician.

Reading Time: _____
Word Count: 285
Reading Speed: _____

Try it again without the focus to guide you. As you read the following passage, keep your focus about 1 to 1¹/₂ inches in from each side. Zero in on the text, not the margins. Keep track of your reading time.

The Computerization of Medical Records

The health care industry is currently moving toward linking institutions through a proposed information infrastructure and communication networks. Linkages would allow the transfer of patient data from one care facility to another to coordinate services, and would allow collation of clinical records for each patient over time among providers and at various health sites to provide a longitudinal record, one that forms a cradle-to-grave view of a patient's health care history. Electronically connecting the health care industry by an integrated system of electronic communication networks would allow any entity within the health care system to exchange information and process transactions with any other entity in the industry.

Smart cards have been proposed as a means to computerize and maintain health care information. Smart cards can function to store information, which can be accessed when a patient presents the card to a health care practitioner, and/or as an access control device, to maintain a more secure and efficient access control system for health care information computer systems.

A major focus of security and confidentiality measures for these systems is preventing privacy invasion by trusted insiders. For on-line computer systems, security is generally provided by the use of user identification names and passwords, and by menus to control access to computer system functions. Some systems also use audio trails to record significant events on a system. However, technology alone cannot completely secure a system. Organizational education, policies, and disciplinary actions supplement technical protection for confidentiality. Smart cards can serve as an access control device, providing the security functions that are normally carried out by the user.

Reading Time:	_____
Word Count:	275
Reading Speed:	_____

Part 3

Dynamic Reading Techniques

In a very real sense, people who have read good literature have lived more than people who cannot or will not read . . . It is not true that we have only one life to live; if we can read, we can live as many more lives and as many kinds of lives as we wish.

—S. I. Hayakawa

What is the meaning of the word *read*? You already know that reading is more than just looking at words—it is receiving and sorting out information from the words. Power readers have learned to adjust *the way they read* to get the most from their reading time. Using the *active reading* techniques in this lesson, you too can make the most of your reading time.

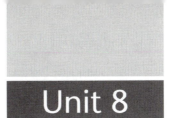

Becoming an Active Reader

The way a book is read—which is to say, the qualities a reader brings to a book—can have as much to do with its worth as anything the author puts into it. . . . Anyone who can read can learn how to read deeply and thus live more fully.

—Norman Cousins

Y ou know that you must be able to read fast to deal with the future. But fast isn't enough. To take charge of the Information Age, you must also be an intelligent reader, one who can read quickly but expertly. This chapter will teach you the best ways to become a more effective reader. You will learn how to:

◆ take charge of your reading

◆ zero in on the main idea *fast*

◆ use proven reading techniques

◆ restate what you read in your own words

◆ make predictions while you read

When you meet an exciting person for the first time, you don't stand back and say, "Entertain me." Instead, you share your experiences, your thoughts, and your dreams. You get involved in the conversation. You ask questions and you listen. You respond and interact in the dialogue. In the process, you often learn as much about yourself as you do about the person.

You create the same exciting relationship with a writer when you read a text—any kind of text. Reading gives you an experience of people, places, and ideas you could rarely get in other ways. You enter into the lives and minds of people who open up whole new worlds.

Reading Is a Dynamic Process

Reading is not a passive activity. It involves more than looking at words. Reading is a dynamic process between the page, the eye, and the brain. Take an active role in your reading right from the start, and you'll improve your understanding of everything you read. Conduct an ongoing dialogue with the reading. Ask yourself these questions:

What Do I Already Know About the Topic?

People write to convey ideas that are important to them and to their audience. They have many ways of doing this; likely one of the most effective is building on the information their readers already have. When you read, your brain actively links what you already know and what is new to you. You understand and learn new material by associating it with information that you already know.

Tap Prior Knowledge

Before you start reading, spend a few minutes writing down what you already know about the topic of the passage. Jot down your opinion of the topic and what information you would like to find out. This process helps you ask the big questions once you begin reading the material. It helps you link what you already know with what you are about to learn. In addition, thinking for yourself before you come under the writer's influence helps you arrive at your own conclusions. This is called *tapping prior knowledge*—connecting your background and personal experience with the writer's viewpoint and experiences.

Jotting down information about what you already know on a topic helps you respond quickly to new material, a crucial step in coping with the information deluge. This is also a valuable skill to use when you are faced with unexpected tests or the need for information you have not studied.

Imagine that you are about to read an article entitled "Leaders of the Future." Take a few minutes right now to jot down what you know about this topic. Then make some notes about what you would like to learn from this article. The whole process shouldn't take you more than five minutes.

◆ What I know about the topic:

_____

◆ What I would like to learn:

_____

Why Am I Reading This?

Think about your *purpose*—your *reason*—for reading a specific book, report, article, or memo. Why have you picked this document to read? You may be reading to:

◆ get facts

◆ get opinions

◆ be entertained

◆ confirm a belief

◆ get an overview on an issue

◆ learn new information

◆ review notes

◆ support a position

Next, think about how much information you need to get from this particular document. If you need specific facts, you can skim the material until you come to the information. Then you will have to read that portion of the text in depth. If you need general opinions or an overview, you can read much more quickly. When you read about a subject that you know well, your brain is familiar with the facts. As a result, you can move quickly through most of the text and slow down only when you come to new information.

Identify Your Purpose

You can slash your reading time by identifying your purpose and focusing on it. Power readers recognize that they can skip parts of a document. Defining your purpose can help you make sure you're getting exactly what you need from your reading.

Try these steps with the following passage. Skim the article and decide why you would read it. Then decide what level of information you need to get from it. Would you read the article quickly or slowly? Why?

The Leaders of the Future

Who will be the leaders of the twenty-first century? They won't be the isolated technocrats so worshipped a decade ago or the hands-on paternalistic bosses of the old days. Neither will they be the slash-and-burn whiz kids who have left their mark on the last ten years.

Here are the skills the new CEOs will have to have to make the cut:

◆ *Global thinkers.* It's been said all over the media, and with good cause. Thinking globally, like the Germans, Japanese, and Koreans, is still not commonplace among American managers, especially among managers in small- and mid-sized businesses. The boss of the future will be in all parts of the globe, not attached to any one segment of it, and possess what the Japanese have called an "equidistant perspective." Increasingly, this will be a requirement of managers at all levels and in all firms.

◆ *Team players.* It's equally important to shed the old idea of firms having fixed borders. The market of the future will be shifting, linked by fiber-optic cables and modems, not brick and mortar. Effective managers will be able to "gather" different employees from the corners of the globe, linking operations through a vast net of technology. When the work is completed, it's time to move with ease and fluidity to another market and another network.

Purpose for reading: _____

Level of information needed: _____

What Information Is Important?

When you read to keep up with the Information Age, you need immediate and current information. Here's how to get to the heart of the matter.

Skim and Scan

Start by skimming the book to identify the main ideas. Focus on the introduction, the table of contents, chapter headings, and opening paragraphs. Also glance at the author's biography. Build on prior knowledge by looking for facts you already know. Read this as quickly as you can. This way, you will be able to focus on the key ideas and critical details and skim over the material that does not pertain to your needs. Try it now with a book of your own.

How Is the Material Organized?

After your preview, think about how the information is presented in the text. Authors arrange their facts, details, and examples to make their point in the most effective way. Here are some ways that information can be arranged in a document:

◆ most to least important

◆ least to most important

◆ cause and effect

◆ advantages and disadvantages

◆ chronological order

◆ spatial order

◆ steps in a process

◆ examples

◆ comparison and contrast

◆ reasons

Zeroing in on the main ideas will help keep you focused on the author's primary points and prevent you from becoming bogged down in minute details. Find the method of organization in the following passage.

Energy-Saving Tips

◆ You may be spending a lot more money than you think on baths and showers. Substantial savings can be achieved without much trouble. There are two ways to do this. The first is to take shorter showers and baths at the lowest acceptable temperature. The second is to install flow restrictors in the showerheads. The restrictors reduce the water flow from six to eight gallons to two to three gallons per minute. The best ones reduce the flow without sacrificing the hard spray that most people like.

◆ When insulating, make sure that you include the attic. It is common to find large openings where pipes, ducts, or exhaust fans are cut through the attic floor. All the obvious holes and gaps can be plugged with the exception of the gaps around recessed light fixtures and vents in the attic. Do not cover light fixtures directly as this may cause a fire.

◆ An inexpensive storm window can be made by attaching polyethylene plastic sheeting (at least 6 millimeters thick) over the windows.

(The passage is organized by examples.)

What Is Coming Next in the Passage?

Reading experts may not agree with each other on everything, but they are all in agreement that a key activity in reading is *making predictions*. As you read, your brain is trying to figure out what is coming next in the text. Once you find out what is coming next, you either confirm or revise your prediction. For example, if you came to a chapter called "Infrastructure Options," your predictions could range from ideas about government positions to guesses about highways in developing countries. As you read on, you confirm your guess to see if you were or were not on target.

Making Predictions Quickly

To be effective, you must make reading predictions quickly—often without being consciously aware of the process. Without predictions, you would have to consider an often limitless range of new information. But by making predictions, you can narrow your focus to reasonable parameters. Learning to make quick and accurate reading predictions greatly improves your speed and comprehension.

If you are reading fiction, identify yourself with the main characters. Think about how the characters' experiences and attitudes are the same as and different from your own. Ask yourself these questions as you make predictions about stories and novels:

1. What has happened in the story thus far?

2. What important event in the story might cause something to happen?

3. What might happen next in the sequence of events?

4. How will the character act next?

What's the Main Idea of This Reading?

To answer this question, restate the information in your own words. Create brief summaries to make sure that you have understood the author's point. Some power readers actually write their summaries on index cards; others create their summaries mentally. Whatever method you use, it's vital that you create your summaries out of your own words. Copying the author's phrases will usually not help you; in many cases, doing this shows that you really don't grasp what you have read.

Organize the Information

Devise different ways to organize the information that is useful to you. These methods will vary depending on the material and your purpose for reading. See what connection you can find among ideas. Use visual aids to help—diagrams, sketches, and flow charts are especially useful ways of extracting the main idea. Some power readers create rhymes, songs, and other word plays to help them distill the key points and remember them. The more you force your brain to organize the material, the better you will be able to understand and recall it. No matter how long the reading is, try to create a summary that is no more than a page long. Go over and over the page until you know it well. This is an especially useful way to prepare for an important test.

What Questions Do I Have?

To read faster and absorb more, "ask" the writer questions as you read. Try to answer the questions—and don't be afraid to guess! For instance, suppose you are reading about the Internet. You see the following terms: *interactive, high-speed, modem, server, e-mail, realtime,* and *CD-ROM*. Here are some questions you might ask yourself:

◆ Which of these terms have I read or heard before?

◆ What does each of these terms mean?

◆ Can I define the unfamiliar terms from their context?

◆ If I still can't figure out what they mean, how could I get their definitions?

As you continue reading, you will discover that some of your answers are right on the mark, some are close, and some missed the target. But whether you are correct all the time or not doesn't matter as much as you may think. Why? Because asking yourself questions and comparing and contrasting your ideas with the text will help you understand what you're reading.

What Do I Want to Get Out of This Text?

In large part, the answer to this question will depend on your purpose for reading. Save your time for the key issues; don't bother focusing on irrelevant facts. In general, you will find about two-thirds of what you need in about one-third of the book.

Now apply the above techniques to the following passage. Write your answers to these questions on a separate sheet of paper. Time yourself to calculate your reading speed.

1. What do I already know about the topic?

2. Why am I reading this?

3. What information is important?

4. How is the material organized?

5. What is coming next in the passage?

6. What's the main idea of this reading?

7. What questions do I have?

8. What do I want to get out of this text?

New Twist on No Fault

No state has adopted a no-fault auto insurance system with restrictions on the right to sue since North Dakota's law took effect on January 1, 1976. But now the long period of inactivity may be drawing to a close. A nationwide campaign is under way to gather support for a new form of no-fault insurance. Its principal author is none other than Jeffrey O'Connell, the law professor largely responsible for popularizing the no-fault concept twenty-five years ago.

The new plan, O'Connell says, is "very different from what we proposed in 1965, in the sense that in '65 we were talking about a scheme for relatively modest no-fault benefits and a relatively modest elimination of tort [injury] suits, because that was what seemed to be feasible at the time. This [current] proposal gives the motorist a choice between buying no-fault or tort liability insurance. And if one chooses to go into the no-fault system, one very largely eliminates one's rights to sue for noneconomic loss for pain and suffering. So, in effect, people who elect the no-fault system are opting out of the tort system except for claims for drunken driving and a few more egregious accidents of that nature."

Project New Start

In late 1988, to promote the concept of "consumer choice" auto insurance, a group of consumer activists set up a nonprofit

organization called Project New Start. For motorists who choose no-fault policies, the group projects an average savings of at least 20 percent from the rates they now pay for minimum coverage. This discount, along with the assurance of prompt payment of accident-related expenses, is expected to be one of the prime attractions of the no-fault option.

Under the model legislation drafted by Project New Start, a motorist with no-fault coverage may not sue another no-fault motorist for accident-related injuries. Instead, both drivers will be compensated for economic losses by their own insurers. Two no-fault drivers involved in the same accident also waive the right to sue for pain and suffering, but they can sue for economic losses that exceed the limits stipulated in their insurance policies.

A motorist who opts for liability coverage under the consumer choice system retains the ability to sue any driver for damages. At the same time, he remains subject to being sued on similar grounds by others. In cases where a no-fault driver and a liability driver are involved in an accident, the no-fault driver turns first to his own insurer for compensation but also is able to sue the liability driver for uncompensated losses (both economic and noneconomic).

Uninsured Drivers

The consumer choice system affords no protection for uninsured drivers, who cannot sue insured motorists except where drunken or drugged driving or intentional infliction of injury is involved. In an accident with an uninsured driver, a driver carrying liability insurance would be compensated for losses by the uninsured motorist's provisions of his own policy. Under the same circumstances, a no-fault driver would also be compensated by his own insurer. Furthermore, both types of insured motorist are free to sue uninsured motorists for both economic and noneconomic damages.

Three Ways to Save Money

Project New Start selected Arizona as its target state for 1990. James L. Brown, a cofounder of Project New Start and director of the Center for Consumer Affairs at the University of Wisconsin at Milwaukee, says there are three areas where enough money could be saved to permit significant reduction of auto insurance rates.

"First," he says, "you can get the money from alleged excessive insurance industry profits. Even the most virulent critics of the automobile insurance industry pretty widely agree that the industry is not excessively profitable now. So that doesn't seem to be a particularly fruitful area for looking for the dollars needed to reduce insurance costs.

"Second, you can try to get some of those dollars by making the industry more efficient. Various consumer organizations are now working to improve the industry's efficiency, and many of these efforts are being supported by industry members.

"Third, you can try to reform the litigation system, the liability system, which is the area that Project New Start is focusing on [by restricting opportunities to sue for pain and suffering]. We feel there is a real potential for squeezing more dollars out of the . . . liability system, so that you get a higher percentage of premium dollar back to victims of auto accidents."

Officials of more than a dozen consumer organizations are members of Project New Start's national committee. Nonetheless, some advocates of insurance reform are bothered by the fact that the consumer choice plan also has considerable support within the auto insurance industry. Harvey Rosenfield, the California insurance reformer, goes so far as to call Project New Start "an insurance industry front." In his view, the campaign for consumer choice insurance is an effort to derail reform efforts modeled on Proposition 103.

Reading Time: _____
Word Count: 750
Reading Speed: _____

Reading for Levels of Meaning

Books: The most effective weapon against intolerance and ignorance.
—Lyndon Baines Johnson

When you read, the full meaning of a text emerges on three levels: the literal, the inferential, and the evaluative. Most people read at only the first two levels; power readers, however, are those people who have learned to read at all three levels at the same time. Here's how it's done.

How to Read for Levels of Meaning

Look for the literal meaning.

- ◆ Read exactly what the words say. Find out what the author directly states in the text.

Find the inferential meaning.

- ◆ An *inference* is an educated guess about content. You make an inference when you put together what the author states with what you already know. Inferences are scaffolded on direct statements and prior knowledge.

Make the evaluative leap.

- ◆ Evaluations are judgments or decisions about the author's statements. You make evaluations when you decide whether or not you agree with what the author has stated and implied in the text.

Look for the Literal Meaning

When you read for literal meaning, you are taking the author's words at "face value" to understand what the text means. You omit any opinions or judgments about the author's words; instead, you simply scan the text to gather information from it. As you read for literal meaning, you will look for:

◆ important facts

◆ the author's main argument

◆ details about plot

◆ minor details or statements

Here are some questions you should ask yourself as you read for literal meaning:

◆ What are the key facts in this passage?

◆ What point is the author making?

◆ What happens in the story?

◆ What events move the story along?

When you read on a literal level, don't slow down to look up unfamiliar words in the dictionary. Instead, try to use context clues to get a sense of the word's meaning. Look at the surrounding words and phrases for clues. Ask yourself, "What word can I plug in that might mean the same thing as the word I don't understand?"

In the same way, if you don't understand a particular sentence, look to the surrounding sentences for clues. Ask yourself, "How does this sentence follow what I have already read?" Or, you can try to break the confusing sentence down into smaller sentences that you can more easily understand.

Read the following passage on a literal level. Ask yourself, "What point is this author making?" Try to read as quickly as you can.

No longer is it true—as Euripides said it was true in the fourth century B.C.—that "a woman should be good for everything at home, but abroad, good for nothing." For the Peace Corps has already sent abroad several thousand women who are serving in Africa, Asia, and Latin America. Of the volunteers now overseas, one third are women. They are teachers, nurses, home economists, social workers, laboratory technicians, doctors, and rural development workers. The record they are writing, supported by requests from thirty countries for two thousand more like them, proves that Euripedes underestimated the power of a woman—especially a woman in the Peace Corps.

Did you find this literal point: "Women are an important part of the Peace Corps"?

Find the Inferential Meaning

If reading for literal meaning can be said to be reading "on the lines," reading for inferences is reading "between the lines." When you read to find the inferential meaning of a sentence or passage, you are filling in the information not in the text from your memory and experience. Follow this equation:

stated ideas + experience clues = inferences

Inferences can be divided into types, as follows:

Type of Inference	Topic
agent inference	who?
object inference	what?
time inference	when?
location inference	where?
action inference	how?
instrument inference	what tool?
category inference	which group?
cause/effect inference	what reason? what result?
problem/solution inference	what situation? what answer?
feeling/attitude	what emotion?

When you make inferences, you are generalizing about the information you are reading. A generalization is a broad statement or conclusion drawn from information in the text and integrated with prior knowledge. The generalization is "valid" if it is based on sufficient evidence; the generalization is "invalid" if the text contains exceptions to the statement. Making inferences through generalizations can help you figure out things that the writer does not directly tell you.

Use this checklist as you make inferences.

Inference Checklist

✔ What is the literal meaning of this passage?

✔ What is implied rather than stated?

✔ What generalization can I make?

✔ Is the generalization valid or invalid?

✔ What prior information do I need?

✔ What does the author expect me to know?

✔ What clues did I use to make these inferences?

✔ What have I figured out that the writer does not directly state in the passage?

Read the following passage for its literal and inferential meaning. Then answer the questions that follow.

Deal only with a reputable, responsible contractor. Ask for references from people who have used the company. Inspect some installations if possible. Shop around; get estimates from several companies.

◆ Check with your state and local consumer protection offices and Better Business Bureau to see if any complaints have been filed against the contractor.

◆ Watch the advertising claims for saving energy. Make sure the installation will pay for itself within a reasonable period of time.

◆ Do not sign a contract you do not understand. Never sign a blank contract.

◆ Get all guarantees and warranties in writing.

◆ Contracts signed in your home or any place other than the seller's normal place of business are subject to a three-day cooling-off period. This means you have the right to cancel your contract anytime before midnight of the third business day after the contract has been signed. The contractor must provide you with two copies of the cancellation form.

◆ The contractor should provide you with a Certificate of Insurance. This covers workmen's compensation, property damage, and personal liability.

1. What is the literal meaning of this passage?

2. What is implied about contractors?

3. What generalization can you make about consumers from this passage?

4. What prior information does the author expect readers to know?

Answers

1. The passages describes ways that consumers can choose a reputable contractor.

2. The author implies that not all contractors are reputable.

3. Consumers must know and protect their rights.

4. The author expects readers to know something about contractors and the relationship between them and their customers.

Make the Evaluative Leap

If reading for literal meaning is reading "on the lines" and reading for inferences is reading "between the lines," evaluative reading is reading "beyond the lines." Evaluative reading is called critical reading because it calls for higher-order thinking skills such as distinguishing between facts and opinions, evaluating the author's purpose and point of view, and recognizing the impact of an author's tone on the meaning of a passage.

Evaluate Facts and Opinions

When you evaluate the facts and opinions in a passage, you think about what you have read and make a judgment as to whether the passage represents something that can be verified (a fact) or the writer's personal feelings and beliefs (an opinion).

Writers sometimes blur the distinction between facts and opinions to make their arguments more persuasive. They do this by adding an opinion to a fact. This makes the statement seem completely rather than just partially true. Also watch for absolute words such as *all, none, always, never, all the time, continually, not ever*. They often signal that a statement is an opinion rather than a fact.

Power readers can discern the difference between facts and opinions to evaluate the validity of the author's argument. This technique will help you get the most from your reading.

Follow these steps when you evaluate facts and opinions:

1. Look for statements that can be proven.

2. Ask, "Are these statements true?"

3. If both answers are yes, the statement is a fact.

4. If one or both answers are no, the statement is not a fact.

See how good you are at distinguishing between facts and opinions by labeling each of these statements F for fact or O for opinion.

_____ **1.** An illegal alien is a foreign national who has entered the United States surreptitiously or by fraud or has violated the terms of lawful entry by, for example, overstaying a tourist visa or accepting unauthorized employment.

_____ **2.** The United States has always welcomed tourists in the past.

_____ **3.** Almost 10 million illegal aliens have been apprehended by the Immigration and Naturalization Service (INS) of the U.S. Department of Justice since 1920.

_____ **4.** Quotas were first assigned in the Immigration Act of 1924, which restricted immigration from eastern hemisphere countries to a proportion of the number of persons, of specified national origin, in the United States at the time of the 1920 census.

_____ **5.** Immigrants from eastern hemisphere countries rarely brought the most useful skills with them and usually proved to be problems later on.

_____ **6.** All illegal immigrants compete with native-born American workers for low-wage, low-skill, and low-status jobs.

_____ **7.** Regardless of their nation of origin, illegal aliens employed in professional and managerial work in their home countries were very likely to move down the employment scale to less skilled jobs in the United States.

_____ **8.** More stringent legislation is needed to prevent illegal aliens from taking jobs away from U.S. citizens.

_____ **9.** The typical illegal alien is a young adult, male, economically motivated, and supporting at least one relative or dependent in his country of origin.

_____ **10.** About 63 percent of the illegal aliens who enter the United States from Mexico had been employed in their home country as laborers or service workers.

Answers

1. F	3. F	5. O	7. F	9. F
2. O	4. F	6. O	8. O	10. F

Evaluate Purpose and Point of View

When you evaluate purpose and point of view, you probe the selection to discover why the author wrote it and how he or she feels toward the subject matter. Some selections are written to inform; others, to persuade. Still others, such as novels and short stories, are written to entertain. A selection can have more than one purpose, but one purpose will usually be more important than the others.

Why is it important to evaluate the author's purpose? When you understand the author's purpose, you can adjust your reading rate accordingly. For instance, most people read an informational piece more carefully and slowly than they read an entertainment piece.

Follow these steps when you evaluate purpose and point of view:

1. Read the selection at your fastest speed.

2. Think about why it was written. Ask, "Did the author present facts, try to persuade me, or try to entertain me?"

3. If the selection has multiple purposes, decide which one is most important.

4. Then ask, "What is the author's opinion of the topic? What words and phrases reveal the author's viewpoint?"

5. Make your evaluation by deciding whether you agree or disagree with the author.

Read the following passage to evaluate the author's purpose and point of view.

The Changing Nature of the Property Tax

When the property tax came into existence in the United States it was a relatively progressive tax. However, over the years the property tax has become less progressive. Today it is a relatively regressive tax.

When the property tax was instituted, most wealth in the United States was in the form of real property. Therefore, the property tax was basically a tax on wealth, and thus progressive. Wealthy landowners would pay a tax proportionate to the value of their real property holdings, while the less affluent, who usually owned an insignificant amount of land, would pay little, if anything.

As time went on, new forms of wealth became more important. Intangible wealth, such as stocks and bonds, as well as personal property, such as cars and yachts, began to account for an increasing proportion of the nation's wealth. Today many wealthy people have only a small portion of their assets in real estate, while many lower- and middle-income people have their life savings invested in their homes. Thus, the property tax has become regressive because it is not strongly correlated to the ability to pay. People who have chosen to invest most of their assets in real property are the hardest hit.

The property tax could be made more progressive. For example, the tax could be expanded to encompass personal property such as stocks and bonds. In the United States, 1 percent of the population owns 70 percent of the corporate stock. If this property was taxed, the overall tax rate could be reduced dramatically.

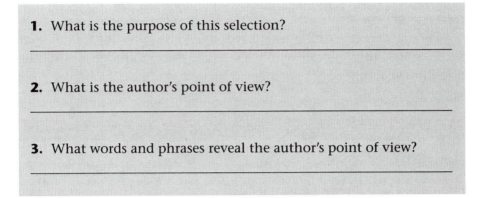

1. What is the purpose of this selection?

_____

2. What is the author's point of view?

_____

3. What words and phrases reveal the author's point of view?

_____

Answers

1. To persuade people to make the property tax more progressive.

2. The author believes that the current property tax is unfair.

3. Examples include the entire final paragraph.

Evaluate Tone

An author's tone is his or her attitude toward the subject matter. The tone can be serious, furious, ironic, humorous, or sarcastic, for example. It can be emotional or moderate, reasonable or irrational. When you evaluate tone, read between the lines to find clues about how the writer feels about the subject.

Read the following excerpt from Thomas Paine's "The Crisis," published in 1776, and decide which words best describe Paine's tone.

My own line of reasoning is to myself as straight and clear as a ray of light. Not all the treasures of the world, so far as I could believe, could have induced me to support an offensive war, for I think it murder; but if a thief breaks into my house, burns and destroys my property, and kills or threatens to kill me, or those that are in it, and to "bind me in all cases whatsoever," to his absolute will, am I to suffer it? What signifies it to me, whether he who does it is a king or a common man; my countryman, or not my countryman; whether it be done by an individual villain or an army of them? If we reason to the root of things we shall find no difference: neither can any just cause be assigned why we should punish in the one case and pardon in the other.

Did you describe the tone as angry, irate, or inflammatory? If so, you understand how to evaluate a selection to find the author's tone.

Put together everything you have learned about reading for different levels of meaning by reading the following passage and answering the questions that follow.

Taxing Mail-Order Purchases

In their never-ending quest for additional revenue, state and local governments have targeted mail-order purchases as a potentially lucrative source of tax revenue. It's easy to see why: By some estimates, merchandise ordered by mail or through toll-free numbers and television shopping networks now accounts for about 20 percent of all retail sales in the United States. The National Association of State Budget Officers (NASBO) calculates that states and localities with sales taxes would collect nearly $3 billion if all such transactions were taxed.

The trouble is, a 1967 Supreme Court ruling seemed to place mail-order sales off limits to state and local tax authorities. The case, *National Bellas Hess Inc. v. Department of Revenue of the State of Illinois*, involved an attempt by Illinois to require a Missouri-based mail-order house to collect and remit the state "use tax." This type of levy, routinely imposed by states with sales taxes, applies to the use in the state of products on which the sales tax has not been paid. Although the tax theoretically covers all products subject to sales taxation, in practice it usually is collected only on big-ticket consumer items like automobiles and boats, which are registered at the time of purchase.

In finding for National Bellas Hess, the mail-order house, the Supreme Court was swayed by the fact that the company had no physical presence in Illinois, employed no sales agents there, and did not advertise in the Illinois media. "All of the contacts which National does have with the state," the court observed, "are via the United States mail or common carrier." And this, the court concluded, did not constitute a sufficient "nexus"—defined as "some definite link, some minimum connection, between a state and the person, property or transaction it seeks to tax."

In an effort to bypass the National Bellas Hess decision, state and local government organizations banded together last year to press for passage of federal legislation permitting mail-order purchases to be taxed. But local officials withdrew their support when they found that the bill, sponsored by Rep. Jack Brooks, D-Texas, did not contain language assuring local governments of a share of the tax proceeds.

The states, meanwhile, have seized the initiative. According to the Direct Marketing Association, a trade group, twenty-eight states now levy sales taxes on mail orders from out of state. They imposed the taxes because increasing numbers of mail-order houses now have a "nexus" in many states and thus are no longer protected by National Bellas Hess.

A key point of contention between supporters and opponents of mail-order taxation concerns the problems that mail-order houses would face in complying with the sales tax laws of hundreds of state and local governments. The task is "complex and expensive," according to attorney Jerome A. Geis of St. Paul, Minnesota, "since each taxing unit has different rates, different product and purchaser exemptions, variant filing requirements, and dissimilar audit and enforcement procedures. These extraordinary compliance costs are estimated to be 15 cents for every $1 of use tax collected, which compares to 1 to 3 cents for every $1 of tax collected by an in-state retailer."

Marcia Howard, research director for NASBO, believes the collection problem is less daunting than Geis indicates. According to Howard, computer software now on the market can perform the tax calculations on phoned-in orders with relative ease. But difficulties can arise, she acknowledges, "when I, for example, fill out a form and mail it in, and it's up to me to figure out whether or not I owe the sales tax and if I do, how much it is. Mistakes can be made, and that's a legitimate concern."

Reading Time: _____
Word Count: 560
Reading Speed: _____

1. On a literal level, this passage describes

2. What is implied about state and local governments?

3. What generalization can you make about mail-order houses from this passage?

4. What prior information does the author expect readers to know?

5. Is the following statement from the passage a fact or an opinion? "The National Association of State Budget Officers (NASBO) calculates that states and localities with sales taxes would collect nearly $3 billion if all such transactions were taxed."

6. What is the purpose of this selection?

7. What is the author's point of view?

8. What words and phrases revealed the author's point of view?

Answers

1. Taxing mail-order purchases.
2. They are always alert for new ways to gain revenue.
3. Their business is booming.
4. The definition of a mail-order business.
5. Fact.
6. To inform.
7. Neutral.
8. Examples will vary

Unit 10

Finding the Topic Sentence

The multitude of books is making us ignorant.

—Voltaire

Power readers get the point of a passage *fast.* "How do they do it?" you may ask. One of the most effective methods they have discovered is finding the main idea in each paragraph. They do this by looking for the key sentence in each paragraph—the *topic sentence.*

The topic sentence states the primary point in each paragraph. Topic sentences are general statements about the content of the paragraph. They telegraph the information the paragraph contains by giving you an overview of it. The writer then backs up each topic sentence with specific details and examples. Once you find the topic sentence, you'll have the gist of the paragraph. If time is short, you can skip most of the details that surround the topic sentence. Finding the topic sentence helps you vary your reading speed to suit your needs.

Here are some sample topic sentences:

♦ On Long Island, there are thirty biotechnology companies employing 3,100 people, according to the New York Biotechnology Association.

♦ The next generation of portable telephones are being developed to offer better service and have a greater range than cordless telephones and consume less power and be less expensive than cellular telephones.

♦ The Consumer Price Index for the Los Angeles and southern California area rose 0.9 percent in February, the regional commissioner of Labor Statistics reported today.

♦ Wireless voice and data communications technologies will affect businesses in the 1990s with an impact rivaling that of the personal computer in the 1980s.

Position in the Paragraph

Because it contains the main idea, the topic sentence focuses on and controls what is written in the paragraph. The topic sentence most often appears in the beginning of a paragraph. However, it can appear anywhere in a paragraph, even in the middle or the end of it. Its position often depends on the type of writing. Consult this table for guidelines:

Type of Writing	Position of Topic Sentence
writing that informs	first
writing that persuades	first or last
writing that entertains	middle or last

Study the following three examples:

Topic sentence at the beginning of a paragraph

<u>Assuming that safety considerations have been designed into the product, some sort of quality control program must see to it that the actual product conforms to the design</u>. An inspection program must weed out the mistakes before they get to market. "Unfortunately," says an Indiana University product safety study, "many manufacturers are reluctant to incur the time and expense needed for a strong self-policing system. Unless they are willing to do this, faulty products will continue to reach the consumer."

Topic sentence in the middle of a paragraph

"If we want to develop energy independence and a benign effect on the environment, then we should do as nature does—use the sun, wind, and hydrogen gas," says Fred Ruiz, a renewable energy advocate. <u>Solar and other alternatives will one day not only meet all our energy needs, but will also supply cheaper power to the United States</u>. This is the belief of many of today's most promising entrepreneurs and researchers, those men and women now exploring new energy technologies.

Topic sentence at the end of a paragraph

Since magnetic tapes and disk drives do not survive being constantly vibrated or sprayed with oil, the idea of using programmable memory chips as memory modules developed. Because PC cards have no moving or loose parts, they are better suited than are standard disk or magnetic tape drives to the jostles of a daily commute. <u>A decade after the first battery-backed memory cards were introduced, their size shrank to that of a credit card, and their success was almost guaranteed as a result of their usefulness.</u>

◆ ◆ ◆ ◆

Test Your Skill

Now apply what you have learned about topic sentences. Read the following paragraphs as quickly as you can. Then underline the topic sentence in each one.

1. With every new notebook, subnotebook, and palmtop computer that is sold, an electronic revolution gains momentum: personal computer (PC) card technology. What was virtually nonexistent technology only a few years ago is now standard on most portable computers. And, the PC card manufacturers say, this is only the beginning.

2. Before you begin any exercise program, it is advisable to have a medical checkup. If you have not had an examination in the past year, if you are past thirty, if you are overweight, or if you have a history of high blood pressure or heart trouble, such an examination may help you avoid extremely serious consequences.

3. The aggression-promoting effects of alcohol are strongest in animals with high blood levels of testosterone, the principal male hormone that distinguishes males from females; humans may or may not exhibit the same pattern. A study of violent Finnish alcohol abusers suggests that the alcohol–violence link may be associated with abnormally low levels of blood sugar (that is, hypoglycemia) and of metabolites of the brain chemical serotonin. Another study suggests that the alcohol–violence link is especially strong in people who exhibit certain abnormal brain wave patterns, both at rest and while responding to outside stresses. Researchers concluded that individual humans and animals deviate widely from expected reactions to psychoactive substances.

4. Cuba is in many respects the source of Central America's problems. It is Fidel Castro's Cuba, of course, that the Sandinistas have modeled themselves upon politically and militarily. As

communist regimes throughout the world are being repudiated by their own citizenry, it is highly ironic that Castro remains dinosaur-like—able to resist in his own domain the changes sweeping the rest of the world.

5. Available evidence suggests that insurance coverage will increase the use of preventative care services, but not to optimal levels. Insurance for preventative care is provided primarily to encourage the use of preventive interventions, rather than to protect against the risk of catastrophic medical costs. Whether insurance coverage or some additional or other means should be used to help encourage the use of clinical preventive services is in part a scientific question.

6. In view of the significant changes in the way that space activities will be carried on in the future, NASA may well have to make certain fundamental shifts in attitude and operation. In the past, it has been NASA's responsibility to meet any given national space objective by itself; in the future, it should be NASA's responsibility to see that the objective is met. That is, NASA should now aspire to a much broader role of seeing that others in our private sector and throughout the world do much more of what it does today.

7. Though most Americans tend to see themselves as highly taxed, Americans generally have less to complain about than people in other developed countries. Among the 23 major industrialized countries belonging to the Organization for Economic Cooperation and Development (OECD), the United States had the second-lightest overall tax burden as a percentage of gross domestic product in the most recent year for which complete data are available. The highest-taxed countries were, in descending order, Sweden, Denmark, Norway, the Netherlands, and Belgium. Bringing up the rear were Portugal, Australia, Japan, the United States, and Turkey.

8. People who drink in bars where fights frequently break out may behave violently in order to "fit in" or to advance socially. People who experience anger or frustration may seek out such settings because they believe that drinking in these types of establishments means social permission to engage in violent behavior. One study of a group of young men who were observed during an

evening of drinking illustrates this by suggesting that drinking patterns and situation influences may play off each other. As the evening progressed, the group began both to behave more aggressively and to move on to establishments where aggressive behavior was more socially acceptable. Just what characteristics of a drinking place make it a magnet for violence are not precisely known, but there is supporting evidence for each of these explanations.

9. Examples of clinical preventative services that evidence shows are effective include: screening for breast cancer (mammography and clinical breast examinations) in women fifty years of age or older; screening for cervical cancer (Pap smears) for women who are or who have been sexually active; cholesterol screening for certain individuals; selected smoking cessation interventions; hypertension screening for certain individuals; adult immunization for certain individuals; and screening for sexually transmitted diseases for certain individuals. Although these services are effective—in the sense that they are likely to result in net benefits to health—all have been found likely to increase financial costs to society when applied to populations that are only at average risk for the specific condition.

10. Despite protective federal laws dating back more than 40 years, as recently as 1973 flammable fabrics were held responsible for 150,000 to 250,000 burns annually—including 3,000 to 5,000 deaths. The statistics are all the more shocking because this specific product danger was recognized more than 100 years ago. When Henry Wadsworth Longfellow's wife was burned to death in 1861, *Scientific American* called for "the preparation of ladies' dresses with nonflammable materials."

Answers

1.	first sentence	**6.**	last sentence
2.	first sentence	**7.**	first sentence
3.	last sentence	**8.**	last sentence
4.	last sentence	**9.**	last sentence
5.	second sentence	**10.**	first sentence

Predicate Power!

Power readers know that the words that create the focus and control the ideas most often appear in the sentence's *predicate*. The predicate is the part of the sentence that contains the verb. The predicate tells what the subject is doing or experiencing. It can also tell what is being done to the subject. In most cases, the predicate will be at the end of the sentence. Knowing that you have to focus on only one part of the topic sentence can also greatly speed up your reading rate and comprehension. Underline the predicate in the following sample sentences:

1. The car phone rang and startled everyone in the vehicle.
2. Two other widely used taxes are regressive.
3. Many in-flight medical problems occur when the plane's environment aggravates preexisting health disorders.
4. The really interesting advances in computers are going to be in software development.
5. Computers have made our lives more complicated, not simpler.
6. Up until now, it has been the scientists who were using the supercomputer.
7. Over the next ten years, the quantity of information on a computer chip will increase by a factor of 1,000 or more.
8. Under the time limitation provisions of the Act, a claim for disability compensation is barred if it is not filed within five years after the injury.
9. The term *injury* includes disease caused by employment.
10. The appellant was employed as an airplane pilot.

Answers

1. The car phone <u>rang and startled everyone in the vehicle</u>.
2. Two other widely used taxes <u>are regressive</u>.
3. Many in-flight medical problems <u>occur when the plane's environment aggravates preexisting health disorders</u>.
4. The really interesting advances in computers <u>are going to be in software development</u>.

5. Computers <u>have made our lives more complicated, not simpler.</u>

6. Up until now, it <u>has been the scientists who were using the supercomputer.</u>

7. Over the next ten years, the quantity of information on a computer chip <u>will increase by a factor of 1,000 or more.</u>

8. Under the time limitation provisions of the Act, a claim for disability compensation <u>is barred if it is not filed within five years after the injury.</u>

9. The term *injury* <u>includes disease caused by employment.</u>

10. The appellant <u>was employed as an airplane pilot.</u>

The topic sentences in the following article have been underlined to highlight them for you. Read through the article, pausing at each topic sentence. Focus on the predicate, usually the last part of the sentence.

Lyme Disease

<u>Lyme disease was first recognized in 1975 after researchers investigated why an unusually large number of children were being diagnosed with juvenile rheumatoid arthritis in Lyme and two neighboring towns.</u> The investigators discovered that most of the affected children lived near wooded areas likely to harbor ticks. They also found that the children's first symptoms typically started in the summer months, coinciding with the height of the tick season. Several of the patients interviewed reported having a skin rash before developing their arthritis, and many also recalled being bitten by a tick at the rash site.

<u>Further investigations resulted in the discovery that tiny deer ticks infected with the spiral-shaped bacterium or spirochete (which was later named *Borrelia burgdorferi*) were responsible for the outbreak of arthritis in Lyme.</u>

<u>In Europe, a skin rash similar to that of Lyme disease had been described in medical literature dating back to the turn of the century.</u> Lyme disease may have spread from Europe to the United States in the early 1900s but only recently became common enough to be detected.

The recent resurgence of the deer population in the Northeast and the influx of suburban developments in rural areas where deer ticks are commonly found have probably contributed to the disease's rising prevalence. <u>The ticks most commonly infected with *B. burgdorferi* usually feed and mate off deer during part of their life cycle.</u>

<u>The number of reported cases of Lyme disease, as well as the number of geographic areas in which it is found, has been increasing.</u> Lyme disease has been reported in nearly all states in this country, although most cases are concentrated in the coastal Northeast, mid-Atlantic states, Wisconsin, Minnesota, and northern California. Lyme disease is endemic in large areas of Asia and Europe. Recent reports suggest that it is present in South America, too.

<u>In most people, the first symptom of Lyme disease is a red rash known as *erythema migrans*.</u> The telltale rash starts as a small red spot that expands over a period of days or weeks, forming a circular, triangular, or oval-shaped rash. Sometimes the rash resembles a bull's eye because it appears as a red ring surrounding a clear central area. The rash, which can range in size from that of a dime to the entire width of a person's back, appears within a few weeks of a tick bite and usually occurs at the site of a bite. As infection spreads, several rashes can appear at different sites on the body.

◆ ◆ ◆ ◆

As you read the following sample passage, skim each paragraph to find the topic sentence. Remember: In most cases, it will be in the beginning of the paragraph. Then slow your pace and read that sentence carefully. Speed back up and skim over the details. Time yourself to calculate your reading speed.

How a New British Tax Led to Riots

LONDON—When the last poll tax was introduced in England in 1380, levying a charge of one shilling a head, the peasants revolted: They stormed from Essex and Kent over the London Bridge, surrounded the Tower, and dragged out the chancellor of the exchequer, Simon of Sudbury. At 11 A.M. on June 13, Sudbury and several other treasury officials were beheaded on Tower Green.

The peasants' revolt was a bloody, chaotic mess. It nearly toppled the monarch, Richard II, who quickly abandoned the new tax. No British leader considered such a tax for six hundred years, until Margaret Thatcher came to power in 1979.

Why the Thatcher government would have chosen to collect a tax that once had such disastrous consequences is a question of modern zeal triumphing over political pragmatism. "I'd give the prime Minister 10 out of 10 for bravery," says Tony Travers, director of research for the London School of Economics, "but not 10 out of 10 for thinking through the consequences."

The poll tax—or, to use the government's term, the community charge—is a flat levy on each adult over the age of eighteen. The more adults who live together, the more the household pays. The poll tax replaced what were called the "household rates"—the property tax collected for community services provided by local councils. The household rates also were detested; as an old saying went, "A man pays his income tax in sorrow, but his rates in anger."

Indeed, there was near universal agreement that the household rates were inequitable and that the whole system needed an overhaul. It was a task that particularly appealed to the Conservatives. The party's October 1974 manifesto boasted: "Within the normal lifetime of a Parliament we shall abolish the domestic rating systems and replace it by taxes more broadly based and related to peoples' ability to pay."

But coming up with a more equitable tax wasn't easy. A local sales tax was considered, but that likely would have sent consumers driving from one area to the next. A new local income tax was proposed, but that was anathema to the Conservatives. The only viable alternative seemed to be the poll tax, which even Margaret Thatcher thought might bring great upheaval. Nonetheless, by the time she became prime minister, abolishing the household rates and replacing them with a poll tax had become her cause.

Under the poll tax system, nearly everyone pays; the tax rolls doubled from 18 million to 36 million people. Property owners no longer passed their taxes to renters (a proportionally small number in Britain, where all but 35 percent of the population owns its housing); renters paid themselves. But, in fact, renters often paid more than homeowners, since there were more adults per household in lower-income groups. And the tax came as a shocking new expense.

Because it taxes people, not property, there were mutters that "the duke alone in his mansion will pay less than the butler and his wife who work for him." That, unfortunately, is the verity of the poll tax.

There were early signs that this sort of "fairness" would cause controversy. Prime Minister Thatcher first enacted the poll tax in 1985 as a reform in Scotland, where a property reassessment had caused the household rates to soar. But, almost immediately, the Scottish cure seemed worse than the problem. Private Tory polls indicated that the Scots were frightened of the poll tax, and when eleven out of thirty-two Tory seats were lost in local elections, the poll tax got the blame. At this point, a more prudent politician might have hesitated. But Margaret Thatcher pressed on, although the Tories added a safety net, in the form of a rebate for the very poorest citizens.

Reading Time:
Word Count: 550
Reading Speed:

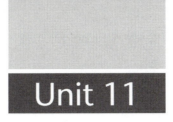

Unit 11

Using Survey, Question, Read, Recite, and Review

Reading is to the mind what exercise is to the body.

—*Sir Richard Steele*

This multistep method (survey, question, read, recite, and review) takes a little time, but it's time worth spending because it can really boost your comprehension. After some practice, you'll find that you pick up a lot more speed as well.

Let's look at each step in detail.

Survey

Skim the passage before you start reading in depth. Look at these places:

◆ title

◆ headings

◆ illustrations

◆ abstract

◆ first paragraph

◆ last paragraph

◆ diagrams

◆ tables

◆ introduction

As you survey, make *predictions* about the content. Based on your survey, decide what reading speed to use so you can pace yourself appropriately.

Question

As you survey the article, ask questions about the material and what you find. Start by turning the title and headings (if there are any) into questions. Asking questions makes you an active reader, which greatly increases your comprehension. Continue making and adjusting predictions as you question.

Read

Now read the passage as quickly as you can. Slow down for key passages and important ideas; speed up for less crucial information. Decide which passages are the most and least important.

Don't be upset if you have trouble telling which details are the most important. The more you practice with this method, the easier it will be for you to select the material you need to know.

While you read, refer back to the predictions you made in the previous two steps and change them as needed. See where you hit the mark and where you missed.

Recite

After you finish reading, look back over the passage. Instead of rereading, look back at important places, such as the title, headings, and key paragraphs. Summarize the material in your head, reducing what you read to a few sentences. This will help you zero in on the key details and to improve your understanding of what you read. Some people find it helps to recite their summary aloud. See if this works for you.

As you practice, you'll find that you can read larger and larger blocks of text before you stop to recite. At first, you might stop to summarize after every paragraph or two. With practice, however, you should be able to take in a page at a time.

If you find that you're having trouble recalling what you read, take a moment to skim the passage again. It's important to make sure that you understood what you read before you go any further. Do a quick summary and then continue on.

Review

As you review, think back to your predictions. Were they on target? If so, isolate the details you used to make them. If not, where and why did you guess incorrectly? Assessing your predictions and revising your methods will enable you to make more accurate predictions next time.

Use the Survey, Question, Read, Recite, and Review (SQ3R) method with the following article. Don't forget to time yourself to make sure that you are reading as quickly as possible.

Optical Fiber: A Faster Way to Move Information

Although optical fibers are a new invention, the basic technology of transmitting data by using light has a long pedigree. In 1880, Alexander Graham Bell obtained a patent for a "photophone," a device that focused a beam of sunlight on a reflector that vibrated in response to sound waves. The light was aimed at a detector 700 feet away, where the resulting vibrations were converted back to electrical current, which was in turn converted back to sound via a telephone receiver. The device worked, but it was not practical for general use. It required sunlight to work—a cloudy day would mean no communication—and even focused sunlight could not reflect more than 700 feet without dissipating.

Reliable photonic communications rested on two fundamental developments: a source of light strong enough to carry over long distances and a "wave guide" to contain the light so that it would not dissipate and so that it could turn corners. The first breakthrough came in 1960, with the first laser, which provided an intense, focused beam of light. The same year, Bell Labs, a division of AT&T, launched an all-out effort to develop a practical waveguide to direct and contain light transmissions. The first system built by Bell researchers was a tube 8 inches in diameter, with mirrors every 100 meters. The contraption worked, but it was so bulky (and expensive) that it was little more practical than the photophone.

Then, in 1966, two researchers in England—Charles Kao and George Hockham—proposed using glass fibers as a waveguide. Four years later, Corning Glass Works, a U.S. company, produced a glass fiber that could transmit signals with a loss of only 200 decibels per kilometer. This was still too much loss for a practical communications system, but it was good enough to convince researchers that fiber-optic communications was a real possibility.

Yet another major step came in 1971, when researchers at AT&T's Bell Labs produced a small laser that, unlike its predecessors, could operate at room temperature. By 1976, Bell lasers had been engineered to the point where they could be used for hundreds of thousands of hours, and, simultaneously, Corning brought down signal loss to 4 decibels with improvements in fiber materials and manufacturing. The result? The first practical fiber-optic communications system. In 1977 AT&T installed the first commercial fiber-optic telephone line in Chicago.

Long Distance

Today, optical fibers have replaced copper wires in virtually every U.S. telephone line of a mile or longer, and optical fibers are beginning to replace copper on transoceanic cables as well. The reason is simple: Optical fibers can provide more service at less cost than copper.

In fact, the potential capacity of optical fibers in voice and data communication is so great that it can be difficult to grasp. With current equipment, an optical fiber can carry more than 3,800 times as much information as a copper wire. A 72-strand optical-fiber cable, which is less than an inch in diameter, can handle more than a million conversations at once. With 10 lasers sending over a single fiber at different frequencies, the entire *Encyclopaedia Britannica* could be sent in one-tenth of a second.

Many Advantages

Optical fiber also has other advantages over copper. For one thing, it is much lighter. One kilometer of fiber-optic cable weighs about 30 pounds, while one kilometer of copper cable weighs about 200 pounds. The optical cable is also less vulnerable to corrosion and electromagnetic interference, and it is considerably more difficult to tap.

What's more, fiber-optic systems are becoming much more efficient and are expected to continue to do so. Because of improvements in fiber materials and transmission equipment, the National Research Council reported, the distance/carrying capacity of fiber-optic equipment increased by a factor of more than 100 between 1979 and 1988, the rate roughly doubling every year.

Meanwhile, the cost of fiber optics has fallen, too. Economies of scale have brought down the per-mile costs of the cable itself, and when that is coupled with the improvements in fiber materials and transmission equipment, the per-item cost of sending information on a fiber-optic cable is so low that it has become the medium of choice for most types of communications. And U.S. companies are well positioned to thrive in the growing market.

According to the Department of Commerce, U.S. companies have easily dominated the domestic market. AT&T and Corning together account for three-quarters of the optical-fiber market, and AT&T and Collins Defense Communications (a division of Rockwell International Corporation) "are considered industry leaders in transmission equipment," according to a Commerce Department report.

Maintaining the Competitive Edge

There are potential problems on the horizon for U.S. manufacturers, however. The U.S. market for optical fibers—which has represented more than half the world market—is approaching saturation. "Fiber installation in Western Europe and Asia is likely to outpace the United States in the next five years," the Commerce Department reports, adding that within the next year, the U.S. share of the world market should drop to 35 to 40 percent. And as U.S. manufacturers look abroad to maintain sales, their major competition will, too.

Reading Time:	_____
Word Count:	870
Reading Speed:	_____

Here's how one student used this SQ3R method to read the previous article more quickly and thoroughly. Study how the student analyzed the article. Then compare and contrast this analysis to your own reading. How many of these tips could you apply to your own reading strategies?

Survey

"First, I did a quick **survey** of the selection. I started by reading the title—*Optical Fiber: A Faster Way to Move Information.* From this I predicted that the entire article was going to be about the advantages of using fiber optic cable in transmitting information. Then I read the heading *Long Distance* and learned that the following section would deal with the transmission of signals over great distances via fiber-optic cable. The heading *Many Advantages* means that the following paragraph(s) will detail the reasons why fiber optic cable is so useful in moving information. From the final heading, *Maintaining the Competitive Edge,* I can infer that the U.S. might have to struggle to stay on top of the competition.

"Then I skimmed the first paragraph and found out that the article's organization was basically *chronological*—from the past to the present. This tells me to expect that the more recent information about fiber-optic cables would be toward the end of the article.

"I finished with a quick skim of the last paragraph and found out that everyone will be scrambling to find new markets for fiber-optic cable. Since I know a lot about fiber-optic cable, I decided to read the article as quickly as I can."

Question

"Here are some questions I asked myself during my survey:

- ◆ What long distances? From where to where?

- ◆ What are some of the advantages of fiber optic cable?

- ◆ How can the U.S. maintain its competitive edge in this market?

- ◆ How can I use this information?"

Read

"As I read, I looked back at my prediction. Soon, I learned that the entire article was not about the advantages of fiber-optic cable; in fact, the first part traces the history of this technology and the last part talks about world-wide market competition. It's really only the middle of the piece that discusses advantages. As a result, I had to adjust my predictions several times.

"In the same way, I had to revise my questions. The article does not talk about how the U.S. can maintain its competitive edge, only that it will have trouble doing so."

Recite

"When I finished reading each section, I looked up and made a quick summary. For the first section, I came up with this summary:

In 1880, Bell devised the concept of fiber optics but it was not until the invention of the laser in 1960 that light could be concentrated enough to make the idea workable. In 1966, the waveguide was created; in 1976, the first practical fiber-optic communications system was created. A year later, AT&T installed the first commercial fiber-optic telephone line.

I continued summarizing each section. Then I made an overall summary of the passage:

Since 1976, when the first workable fiber optics system was created, fiber optics have proven to be lighter, cheaper, and more efficient than copper wire. High amounts of material can be transmitted with astonishing speed via fiber optics. Today, the U.S. market for optical fibers is nearly saturated and world competition is stiff."

Review

"I looked back to my predictions. I was off because I based my ideas on too narrow a survey—only the title, really. Next time, I'll use more information from my survey of the headings and from skimming of the first and last paragraphs."

◆ ◆ ◆ ◆

Following the student's example, try the SQ3R power reading method on the following passage. Read as quickly as you can, but maintain the "internal dialogue" that will help you maximize your comprehension as you pick up speed. Time yourself to calculate your reading speed.

The Expanding High-Tech Job Market: Myth or Reality?

New entrepreneurial companies make up one of the most exciting and fastest growing sectors of the economy. At least that's what a number of recent reports have said, often supporting the claim with this statistic: Of 20 million jobs newly created in the last decade, 87 percent emerged within firms that were 4 years old or younger. This statistic has also been used to suggest that within this sector lies a vast hidden job market for entry-level workers.

With the goal of developing a hiring profile for new high-tech entrepreneurial organizations, I conducted a study that involved interviewing an administrative officer knowledgeable about hiring practices and one employee in each of thirty companies in the midwestern and southeastern United States. The companies, all ten years old or younger, ranged in size from one to five hundred employees. What follows are observations about these companies drawn from my interviews with their corporate officers.

Locating Companies

Before determining the hiring profiles of these companies, I had to develop a strategy for locating them. To obtain a reasonably similar sample of companies, I chose Edward Hincks' definition of *high technology* and modified it to read as follows: "A high-tech firm is one primarily engaged in making products, and/or rendering services, that embody innovative materials, processes, and technologies."

To locate appropriate companies, I first reviewed library resources such as business-related magazines and current books, but I met with little success because of the general nature of the information. Local and regional business-related publications, such as newspapers and newsletters, furnished more specific information about emerging high-tech companies, but chambers of commerce proved to be the most helpful resource by providing information in the form of directories, publications, and referrals to area high-tech associations. Directories were a good source for identifying companies an absolutely invaluable resource for establishing a network of contacts that resulted in personal referrals to other company executives as well as an invitation to a local chapter meeting of an entrepreneur's network.

Methods for Finding New Hires

When asked how new employees were located, employees most often mentioned contacts, networking, and referrals. However, they generally used multiple strategies, with the type of position available being the determining factor.

A typical employer comment was, "I like to hire someone who is known to someone I know." The importance attached to this strategy was substantiated when employees were questioned about how they found their first job with the company. Fifty-three percent indicated that it was through personal contacts.

More than half the companies used newspaper advertising in some form, despite the feeling that it was not very effective and tended to attract large numbers of unqualified applicants.

Interestingly, only 23 percent of the companies identified human resources/personnel as a separate corporate function. In all other cases, responsibility for hiring was assumed by area managers, mostly on an as-needed basis.

Qualifications Preferred for New Hires
Particular qualifications varied widely among companies, depending on their products and services, short- and long-range corporate plans, job openings, and company structure. When all the preferred qualifications were summarized, however, a remarkably similar profile of the ideal job applicant emerged. The applicant's personality appeared to be a crucial factor since all companies mentioned it in some way, including interpersonal relations, professionalism, personal traits, and attitudes toward work.

Typically, employers said they wanted "someone who always gets to the finish line, excellence in all areas of the person's background, demonstrated initiative, and the entrepreneurial spirit— i.e., it can be done and I can do it."

The interviews indicated that many future job openings in these companies would be for key management personnel or low-level technicians, thus further restricting options for job seekers. Many employers also found it extremely difficult to predict the number of future hires because the number depended on cash flow, contracts, projects, and corporate plans for consolidation or expansion.

The latter finding is particularly significant when you further consider the claim that 87 percent of new jobs created in the 1980s were in companies four years old or younger. It's not completely clear, but that statistic appears to be based on a projection from a study done in the 1970s at MIT. If new employers have difficulty predicting future hires, then how accurate was this study?

Further, the MIT study has been criticized for other reasons. For one thing, it included divisions of large companies in the database as well as consulting businesses run by people who were employed full time in other occupations. In addition, the 87 percent figure referred to jobs created by emerging businesses, which does not mean that 87 percent of those jobs are in emerging businesses, and people have confused the two.

Reading Time: _____
Word Count: 800
Reading Speed: _____

Unit 12

Summarizing to Build Comprehension

The man who does not read good books has no advantage over the man who can't read them.

—Mark Twain

A re you able to condense a passage into your own words? If you can, the chances are that you have understood the author's point. Summarizing is extracting key information and creating a synopsis. When you create a summary, you rephrase what you read in your own words. The skill is important in increasing reading comprehension. Follow these steps to find the key details in a passage:

Power Reading Strategy
Selecting Key Information

1. Read the passage or paragraph at your fastest speed.

2. Ask, "What is this passage about? What is the topic here?"

3. Look for the topic sentence. If you can't find the topic sentence (or the passage doesn't have one), create your own.

4. Decide what information the writer gives about the topic.

5. Sift the details. Ask, "Is this information important enough to remember?"

6. Think about the main ideas in the text. Look back at the information you decided was not important. Recheck your decision.

Distinguishing Between Important and Unimportant Information

Being able to distinguish between important and unimportant information helps readers identify the essential points that should be included in a summary. Mastering this skill helps readers know which details to include and which ones to omit.

Read the following passage and the analysis after it.

A Revolution in the Office

In recent years, automatic machinery has revolutionized the operation of the factory, the office, and even the classroom. The large-scale use of automatic equipment in factories is responsible for the great strides made by the electronic industry. Without such mechanization, the total labor force available to specialized industry today could not produce the great volume of goods needed by industry, the public, commerce, and the armed services.

The revolution has been as marked in the office. In addition to relatively simple electronic typewriters and word processors, copiers and complex PCs make office work much simpler and faster for harried supervisors and managers and an overworked support staff. Automated office equipment expedites all type types of paperwork, such as filing, recording, analyzing, and estimating; further, it does the work more economically and accurately.

Finally, in the classroom, machines have streamlined the learning process in many respects. Televisions, CD players, film projectors, videocassette recorders, and tape recorders make more exciting kinds of lectures and demonstrations possible in the huge classes of many colleges and universities. Even in small schools, where enrollments are limited, these same audiovisual aids, when they are properly controlled, allow students to learn materials at their own pace. As a result, more advanced learners are able to move ahead and less advanced students can obtain the extra practice they need.

◆ "What is this passage about? What is the topic here?"

This writer is discussing how automatic machinery has changed the way the factory, office, and classroom are run. The topic is the changes that automation has brought about in these three areas.

◆ Look for the topic sentence.

The topic sentence is in the beginning of the passage: <u>In recent years, automatic machinery has revolutionized the operation of the factory, the office, and even the classroom.</u>

◆ Decide what information the writer gives about the topic.

Factory: automatic equipment in factories equals great progress by the electronic industry. This results in goods needed by industry, the public, commerce, and the armed services.

Office: electronic typewriters, word processors, copiers, and PCs make office work simpler and faster. Automated office equipment expedites paper work.

Classroom: machines have streamlined the learning process and have allowed students to learn at their own pace.

◆ "Is this information important enough to remember?"

What do I have to know from this passage? The most important details list the different machines and the ways they have changed the factory, office, and school. Some of these machines include electronic typewriters, word processors, copiers, and PCs. Some of the ways these machines have changed the workplace and school include expediting all type types of paper work, such as filing, recording, analyzing, and estimating.

◆ Think about the main ideas in the text.

The main idea concerns the ways automatic machinery has made the factory, office, and school more productive.

Creating a Summary

Creating a summary means that you restate what you read in your own words. The original meaning of the passage must be retained and the summary should not include your own opinion of what you read. One easy way to create a summary fast is to answer the reporter's questions, the five *W*'s and *H*: who, what, when, where, why, and how.

As you read the following passage, think about these six questions. A summary is provided.

Some state, county, and municipal records have great value for genealogists. Records of births and deaths may be on file in state bureaus of vital statistics, or they may be kept by a county or municipal official—usually the county, city, or town clerk. Many state governments made no attempt before the twentieth century to centralize vital records. Marriage and divorce records are usually filed with an official of the county in which the marriage or divorce occurred or the state official having custody of vital records. In some instances, however, marriage records are kept in the office of a town of city official. The Superintendent of Documents, U.S. Government Printing Office, Washington, DC 20402, sells three helpful leaflets: Where to Write for Birth and Death Records, Where to Write for Marriage Records, and Where to Write for Divorce Records.

Some states have records of military service performed in state or colonial units, state or colonial land transactions affecting individuals, censuses authorized by federal, state, or territorial legislation, and claims for pension and other benefits based on military service. Such records are often deposited in the state archives. If they are not, the state archivist or a comparable official can usually direct an inquirer to them. For information about Confederate pension application files, write to the appropriate official in the capital of the state from which the service was rendered or where the pensioner resided at the time of his death.

In addition to vital records, county records of genealogical interest include wills, records of administration and distribution of estates, deeds, leases, court records relating to orphans and guardianship, and lists of voters and taxpayers. Municipal records of similar interest include tax lists, registers of voters, and court records. For information about such records, write to the appropriate county, town, or city official.

Summary

who?	amateur genealogists
what?	tracing records
when?	during the present
where?	through federal and state archives
why?	to find out about your ancestors
how?	by writing to different agencies

Practice creating your own summaries as you read the following passage. At the end of each paragraph, stop and make a brief summary. When you finish the entire passage, summarize what you have read. Try to keep your summaries to no more than one or two sentences. Time yourself.

Substance Abuse and Aggression

Evidence from research on animals and humans indicates that patterns of substance abuse and aggressive behavior reinforce each other. It cannot be said that one "causes" the other. For example, alcohol may trigger violent episodes in aggressive animals and people, but rarely in submissive ones.

Patterns of aggressive behavior and substance abuse often become intertwined starting in childhood. Early childhood aggression is a predictor of later heavy drinking, and the combination is associated with an above average risk of adult violent behavior, especially among those who also abuse other psychoactive drugs.

Possible Explanations

Research suggests at least four possible explanations for the link between substance abuse and violent behavior in adolescents. First, adolescents may chronically use psychoactive substances to help them temporarily escape from feelings of rage, guilt, worthlessness, or depression—emotions that often precede aggressive behavior. Second, repeated family arguments over teenage substance abuse may eventually take on a violent character. Next, underlying family problems or socially expected responses may lead some adolescent males to patterns of heavy drinking and fighting as ways to demonstrate their masculinity. Last, boys who regularly observe older males fighting while drinking may expect that violent behavior accompanies alcohol use. All of these processes may be at work, but their roles, interactions, and importance as explanations have not yet been sorted out.

Preexisting psychosis appears to account for occasional violent outbursts by people who are under the influence of amphetamines or hallucinogens, especially PCP. While these drugs are well known to cause disorganized, bizarre behavior, they trigger violence in very few people who are not also psychotic. In studies of laboratory mice and monkeys, bizarre behavior on the part of animals under the influence of PCP fairly commonly provokes violent attacks by others in the group. Anecdotal information and newspaper accounts report similar attacks on humans using alcohol, amphetamines, powdered cocaine, or LSD, but this relationship has not been systematically studied in humans.

Encounters Between People

In a variety of ways, alcohol and drugs modify encounters between people in ways that make these substances greater hazards for violence. In the case of alcohol, these hazards tend to be related to use, while for illegal psychoactive drugs they tend to be related to distribution and purchase.

Some therapists who treat violent sex offenders have reported that their patients tend to have both histories of alcohol abuse and high levels of testosterone. However, these clinical observations cannot demonstrate that alcohol abuse or high testosterone levels cause sexual violence. Studies of many animal species suggest a causal connection—that alcohol reduces testosterone levels but has stronger aggressive-promoting effects in individual high-testosterone animals. However, the relationship has not yet been tested in humans. The frequent involvement of alcohol in acquaintance rapes suggests that social expectations may also be at work: that is, young men who expect to have sex after drinking may try to satisfy their expectations, sometimes forcibly if they encounter resistance.

Reading Time: _____
Word Count: 500
Reading Speed: _____

Part 4

Reading Business Letters and Memos

Every man who knows how to read has it in his power to magnify himself, to multiply the ways in which he exists, to make his life full, significant, and interesting.

—Aldous Huxley

E-mail, faxes, modems, and various on-line services have made it easier than ever to send and receive business letters and memos. If you're a busy manager, this is both good and bad news. On one hand, electronic mail allows for the rapid creation and distribution of business correspondence. On the other hand, these new lanes on the Information Superhighway encourage even more business communications that must be read and answered. Whether your letters and memos arrive via the Internet or the mail clerk, this chapter will show you how to read and digest any business communication quickly and thoroughly.

Finding Key Words and Details

Runyon's Law: The race is not always to the swift, nor the battle to the strong, but that's the way to bet.

—Damon Runyon

Business letters are usually short communications written to give information, to create good will, or to establish a basis for decisions or dealings. A *memo* can also serve a number of different purposes. For example, it can call for action—or document action. Memos can provide brief, informal reports or give a written record of a meeting. They might transcribe a conversation, set up a meeting, or confirm an appointment.

One of the best ways to get what you need from a business communication—*fast!*—is to find *key words*. How can you find out which words are most important? First look for words that name people, places, and things. Then find words that show action.

To see what we mean, read the following sentence. As you read, locate the words that identify people and their actions.

In early 1993, Spectrum sought an injunction against another cellular-equipped modem manufacturer, Data Race.

Did you find these words that name people, places, or things: *Spectrum, injunction, modem manufacturer, Data Race*? Did you find this word that describes an action: *sought*?

Now read just the key words:

Spectrum sought…injunction…modem manufacturer…Data Race.

Notice how your mind is able to fill in the missing words so that you get the main idea of the sentence much more quickly.

Now try locating the key words in the following sentences. Look for words that name people, places, or things. Find the words that tell about actions. Underline all these words.

Exercise

1. The wireless computer market currently has 600,000 users.

2. The company's wireless data transmission technology uses an error-correction protocol.

3. This permits reliable transmission of electronic data between two computers over cellular telephone networks and other wireless communication systems.

4. Today, Liuski International announced its first venture in software distribution in partnership with Computer Associates.

5. Liuski will sell 486 Intel-based Magitronic PCs bundled with CA software.

6. At the same time, Liuski announced record high sales for the current fiscal year.

7. They posted an increase of 55 percent to $212 million.

8. Further, they anticipate an increase in net income of 65 percent for the upcoming year.

9. Liuski is based on Long Island, New York.

10. They distribute microcomputer peripherals and components.

Suggested Answers

1. wireless computer market   has   600,000 users

2. wireless data transmission technology   uses   error-correction protocol

3. transmission   electronic data computers   cellular telephone networks   wireless communication systems

4. Liuski International   announced   venture   software distribution partnership   Computer Associates

5. Liuski   sell   486 Intel-based Magitronic PCs   bundled   CA software

6. Liuski   announced   high sales   current fiscal year

7. They   posted increase   55 percent $212 million

8. they   anticipate   increase   net income
65 percent   upcoming year.

9. Liuski   based   Long Island, New York

10. They   distribute   microcomputer peripherals
components

Using the Cloze Method

Finding key details is so important to powerful reading that it is often used as the basis for a reading test. It's called the *cloze test* and it shows how your mind skips words and creates meaning when you are reading fast. To test your comprehension of details, the test makers omit words that name people, places, ideas, and actions from the passage. All of the missing details are written on a list. Readers have to pick the best word from the list and place it in the passage. How can you figure out what word is missing? It's like completing a jigsaw puzzle. When you complete a puzzle, you look for pieces with the same shapes. When you complete a cloze test, look for surrounding words that express the same ideas. Here's a sample cloze exercise:

Today, Cheyenne Software's new management team is pursuing a vision to create the "mobile office" with a strategy that not only seeks aggressive patent protection and litigation, _____ the total integration of its three subsidiaries, _____ R&D, Marketing and Service, and Distribution.

◆   ◆   ◆   ◆

Did you fill in *but also* in the first blank and a word that means "joining" in the second blank? There, you might have written *linking or connecting*. This shows how your mind works more quickly than your eyes to fill in key details. Try your hand with the following cloze exercise.

Exercise

Directions: Read each sentence as quickly as you can. Try not to pause or look up from the paper. After each sentence, you will find two choices. Select the choice that best completes each sentence.

1. There's not a _____ in the country that doesn't want to be America's biotech capital.

state   person

2. The hottest buzz in the _____ right now is the $30 million bond issued by Rhode Island to build a manufacturing plant for a Massachusetts company.

center   industry

3. What's so _____ about this? The company's lead product is years away from completion.

amazing   calm

4. With this kind of intense _____, how can states position themselves for success on the biotech road?

competition   cooperation

5. Fortunately, with biotechnology development, there is a different way to look at the _____.

strongest   situation

6. Instead of bringing in existing firms from other regions, there is a better way to get the jump on the competition: _____ new companies.

nurture   import

7. In biotech, there's a new answer to the traditional question, "Which came first: the chicken or the _____?"

invention   egg

8. The answer: The _____ that lays the golden eggs.

chicken   goose

9. Biotech companies are confronted with one-of-a-kind _____.

poultry   challenges

10. Most analysts agree that _____ form the heart of any biotech company.

scientists   customers

Answers

1. state	5. situation	8. goose
2. industry	6. nurture	9. challenges
3. amazing	7. egg	10. scientists
4. cooperation		

Exercise

Complete the memo by selecting the best word from the list below and adding it to each sentence. Again, read at your maximum speed to force your mind to fill in the missing words.

strongest	marketing
superlative	factors
locale	people
atmosphere	excellence
shame	half

This is where (**1**) _____ get the idea that all you need to create a (**2**)_____ university is a bubbling biotech center. It's a (**3**) _____ but it does not work that way. New York, for example, is one of the (**4**) _____ research centers in the country but has a doleful lack of biotech companies. How can you convince the movers and shakers that your (**5**) _____ is right for a biotech center?

Internal Synergy

It appears that the key factor is the (**6**) _____ in a university, the feeling the people have about each other and their work. It seems that scientific (**7**) _____ has a relatively small role to play with the success of a biotech firm. One of the best signals is how much attention has been lavished on the technology transfer office. Successful efforts include attention to both internal and external (**8**) _____. Potential investors have to understand the synergistic interplay of timing, value, and impact of patterns. Speed is one of the prime (**9**) _____. It's OK if the first critical licensing deal takes more than six months to wrap up—but the next one better be done in (**10**) _____ the time.

Answers

1. people	6. atmosphere
2. superlative	7. excellence
3. shame	8. marketing
4. strongest	9. factors
5. locale	10. half

Now read the following two business letters, using the techniques you learned in this chapter. Be sure to time yourself and record your reading speed when you finish. Force your eye to concentrate on key words. See if you can pick up speed between the first and second letters.

Harris Roberts
BobRo, Inc.
475 Avenue of the Americas
New York, NY 10019

Dear Harris:

I just spoke to my cousin Alan and he told me that the marketing position at BobRo is open again and that you had suggested that I might have another shot at it. Unfortunately I won't be able to go for it this time. As you can see by the letterhead, my job search was successful. I started at Allied Communications in January as a marketing manager. I am involved in marketing such magazines as *CompAge* and *Country Life* at the newsstand level. It is similar to what I did at J & J and what I would have been doing at BobRo.

Anyway, I wanted to thank you for your help and for thinking of me again. The job at BobRo sounds exciting and I would love to be involved in marketing such products. I plan on building a career at Allied Communications, but please stay in touch (through Alan) about any possible opportunities with your firm. You never know.

Again, thank you very much for your help.

Sincerely,

Lawrence Nicholls

Reading Time:	_____
Word Count:	170
Reading Speed:	_____

DATE: 9/3/95

TO: Jillian Dorans

FROM: Steven Bambinelli

RE: Mktg. Communications Material

CC: Wayne Sausmer, Katie McTigue, Christopher Porcillo

Last week it was discovered that an advertisement for George, Edwards & Conway lingered in the Design Department for several weeks. As a result, we missed a crucial deadline and nearly lost a client. To avoid such delays in the future, the following procedure will now be used to track all projects:

1. Marketing will memo Tom Washington directly on all design matters.

2. The memo will give him all specifications, due dates, and the list of materials he needs to create a piece.

3. Design and Marketing will meet every Thursday morning at 11:00 in the large conference room to discuss all ongoing projects.

4. The administrative assistant will track all projects on the Master Schedule.

Please follow these guidelines to help us keep things running smoothly as we enter the demanding days of the sales meeting, slide show, and redesign of the brochure.

Thanks for your help.

Reading Time: _____

Word Count: 140

Reading Speed: _____

Part 5

Getting the Most from Newspapers

Power Reading Facts

- *There are 1,570 daily newspapers published in the United States.*
- *Their total combined circulation is 60,164,499.*
- *Total Sunday newspaper circulation is 62,159,971.*
- *The biggest selling daily newspaper in America is the* Wall Street Journal, *with a daily circulation of 1,795,206.*
- *The next best selling daily papers are* USA Today *(1,506,708), the* Los Angeles Times *(1,146,631), the* New York Times *(1,145,890), the* Washington Post *(802,057) and the* New York Daily News *(777,129).*

—Editor & Publisher International Yearbook

What does this mean for you? It means that if you're like most Americans, you're reading at least one newspaper a day. It also means that you don't have the time to get all the way through that newspaper—much less through all the other information you have to read. Unit 14 will teach you some invaluable techniques for reading newspapers fast.

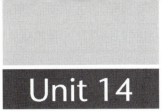

Unit 14

Scanning Newspapers

Along with responsible newspapers we must have responsible readers. No matter how conscientiously the publisher and his associates perform their work, they can only do half the job. Readers must do the rest. The fountain serves no useful purpose if the horse refuses to drink.

—Arthur Hays Sulzberger

Power readers recognize that newspapers have a unique organization. Unlock that organization, and you can get all the news you need to know—in a flash. The three features of a newspaper that you need to know are the *headline*, the *lead*, and the *structure*.

Headline

Newspaper writers and editors know that their readers want to get the facts fast. To help readers decide which articles they want to read, editors preface all articles with a *headline*. Headlines serve to explain the contents of the article and grab the reader's attention. The headlines used in reputable newspapers tend to be informative; those used in tabloids tend to shock. In either case, you can get considerable information from a newspaper's headlines. Here are two examples:

Reputable Newspaper Headline   *Tabloid Headline*

Commandos Kill 4 Hijackers   **Headless Man**
and Rescue 171 Aboard Jet   **in Topless Bar**

Both headlines tell you all about the contents of the article. Even though the second headline has a clever twist, it still tells you all you need to know about the piece. This way, you can decide if the article is worth your reading time. Try your hand on the following ten headlines.

Exercise

Read each of these headlines and decide what each article is about. Then put a check next to the articles you want to read.

_____ **1.** N. Korea Calls Captive U.S. Copter Pilot a Spy

_____ **2.** Some Hurt Cops Don't Get Pensions

_____ **3.** Schools Told of Sex-Case Paroles

_____ **4.** Teen Admits Killings, But Doesn't Say Why

_____ **5.** 4.3 Quake in N. California

_____ **6.** Officer Killed in Car Crash

_____ **7.** Attempted Arson Charge

_____ **8.** Shoppers Find Bargains Galore

_____ **9.** Peso Decline Could Hurt American Exporters

_____ **10.** More Deadly Bullets Are to Be Sold Soon

Answers

1. The article will discuss North Korea's claims that the U.S. pilot they captured is on a spy mission.

2. The article will explain how some injured police officers are denied disability pensions.

3. The article will discuss how officials inform school districts when sex offenders are paroled from prison.

4. The article will discuss a teenager's admission of guilt but not his or her explanation of motive.

5. The article will discuss an earthquake in northern California that registered 4.3 on the Richter scale.

6. The article will discuss how a police officer was killed in an automobile collision.

7. This article will explain how a person was charged with the crime of attempted arson, setting an illegal fire.

8. This article will discuss how the stores are reducing prices, giving shoppers loads of bargains.

9. This article will explain how the decline in the peso will hurt American businesses that export goods.

10. This article will explain about a new, more deadly type of bullet that will soon be available for sale.

Lead

The *lead* is the opening paragraph of a news story. It briefly summarizes the most important features of the event. It tells *Who? What? When? Where? Why? How?* These six questions are called the five *W*'s and *H*. Not every lead will answer every one of these six questions, but every lead *will* give you all the facts you need about the story. If one of the questions is not answered, it is because those facts are not important to the story.

Since all newspaper stories present the most important information in the first sentence, you can skim just the opening paragraph to get all key facts about the story. See what we mean with this sample lead:

4.3 Quake in N. California

At 5:30 this morning, a magnitude 4.3 earthquake 230 miles northwest of San Francisco broke windows, knocked out power, and jolted sleepers awake. No major injuries were reported, but one resident of the area called the quake "a frighteningly strong jolt."

What	When	Where	How
earthquake	5:30 A.M. today	230 miles northwest of San Francisco	jolting sleepers

Exercise

Read each of the following leads. Then complete the chart to tell who, what, when, where, why, and how for each one.

1. Nursing Home Officials Contest Subpoenas

Despite promises to cooperate with state investigators, officials at the Shady Rest Nursing Home are fighting subpoenas requiring them to testify about the fitness of facility director Philip Adams and the planned $5 million expansion of the hospice wing attached to the home.

2. Gasoline Bootleggers Sentenced to Prison

Four men with ties to organized crime who got captured last month in a federal sting operation run by undercover federal agents have been sentenced to prison for their role in a $50 million gasoline bootlegging scheme, according to the Justice Department in Washington, D.C.

3. Suspected Arsonist Arrested

A Glassy Point man distraught over a custody dispute tried to set a fire in the apartment where his common-law wife and their two children lived, local police reported today.

4. Man Killed in Auto Accident

At 8:55 P.M., Haywood Clifford, a forty-five-year-old salesman, was struck and killed on the corner of Main and Cypress by a 1993 Buick driven by retired welder Aldred LeMuir.

5. American–Japanese Summit

American and Japanese negotiators are to meet today in London for a quickly arranged summit on a number of key trade issues, including automobiles, auto parts, and electronic equipment.

Who?   What?   When?   Where?   Why?   How?

1._____

2._____

3._____

4._____

5._____

Answers

1. Who?   officials at the Shady Rest Nursing Home

What?   fighting subpoenas requiring them to testify about the fitness of the facility director and the planned expansion of the hospice wing attached to the home

When?   now

Where?   nursing home

2. Who?   Four men with who were captured in a federal sting operation

     What?   sentenced to prison

     When?   now

     Where?   Justice Department in Washington, D.C.

     Why?   their role in a $50 million gasoline bootlegging scheme

3. Who?   A Glassy Point man

     What?   tried to set a fire

     Where?   in the apartment where his common-law wife and their two children lived

     When?   today

     Why?   distraught over a custody dispute

4. Who?   Haywood Clifford

     What?   struck and killed

     When?   At 8:55 P.M.

     Where?   on the corner of Main and Cypress

     How?   hit by a car driven by Aldred LeMuir

5. Who?   American and Japanese negotiators

     What?   will meet for a summit

     When?   today

     Where?   London

     Why?   resolve trade issues

Structure

The facts in newspaper articles are organized from *most* to *least important*. The most important information is in the lead; the least important information is at the end. Newspaper writers arrange their facts this way so editors can more easily make article fit the available space; if space is short because of a late-breaking story, all they have to do is lop off material from the end, a paragraph at a time.

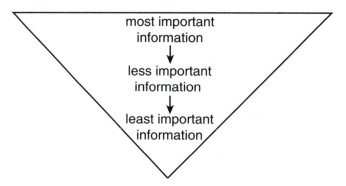

Power Reading Strategies

You can use your knowledge of this organization to speed your reading. Follow these steps:

1. Read the *headline.* Decide if you want to read the article.

2. If you decide to read the article, read the *lead* slowly and carefully.

3. Pick up speed as you continue through the article.

4. Skim the middle of the article.

5. Read the ending only if you are very interested in the story.

Try this technique with the following newspaper article. Time yourself to calculate your reading speed.

 That Lite Stuff

Pickings are no longer slim for dieters these days. The shelves in the diet sections of the supermarket are now groaning under the weight of new products promising good taste but few calories. For today's shedders, there are diet versions of such traditional temptations as cake mixes and syrups, blue cheese salad dressing, pudding, cheese, ice cream, mayonnaise, gravy mixes, and chocolate topping—and, should a thirst develop, even beer and wine.

Diet foods aren't new, but the past few years have seen a striking upsurge in their popularity. Health-conscious Americans seem ready for foods that weigh less heavily on their consciences, and food manufacturers are eager to comply. Many products are marketed as "light" or "lite" versions of regular foods—that is, they contain less of such substances as fat, sugar, or alcohol (in the case of beer and wine), and they are usually lower in calories. The whole idea is so palatable that light foods and beverages are one of the fastest growing segments of the American food industry.

FDA Guidelines

Consumers may wonder whether those streamlined foods really do cut back on the calories. To assure that they do, the Food and Drug Administration requires products claiming low or reduced calories to meet specific limits on calorie content. This helps consumers shopping with weight control in mind to choose products that represent genuine calorie reductions.

Under FDA guidelines, a food can be labeled "low calorie" only if a serving supplies no more than 40 calories and contains no more than 0.4 calories per gram (28.4 grams = 1 ounce). To be labeled "reduced calorie," a food must be at least one-third lower in calorie content than a similar food in which calories are not reduced, and it must not be nutritionally inferior to the unmodified food.

Food that is labeled low or reduced calorie must also bear nutrition labeling. Along with nutrients such as vitamins and minerals, the labels must also give the calories per serving and the serving size to which the figures relate, expressed in identifiable units of measurement such as a cup, slice, teaspoon, or fluid ounce.

Labels of foods that are naturally low in calories, such as mushrooms, are not permitted to use the term "low calorie" immediately before the name of the product. For example, mushrooms could not be labeled "low-calorie mushrooms" because it would suggest that they are lower in calories than other mushrooms. They could be labeled "mushrooms, a low-calorie food."

"Low Calorie" Rules

Even though some foods such as salad dressing are normally eaten in small amounts and provide relatively few calories, they cannot be labeled "low calorie" unless they contain less than 0.4 calories per gram. For example, a typical blue cheese dressing for dieters contains about 40 calories per tablespoon, or 2.5 calories per gram. Thus, it is not low calorie. However, the same dressing could be labeled "reduced calorie" since it has at least one-third fewer calories than regular blue cheese dressing, which has 75 or more calories per tablespoon.

If a food label suggests that calories have been cut, it has to back up that claim with numbers. The label must compare the reduced-calorie food with the unmodified version of the product, such as "reduced-calorie fruit cocktail, 40 calories per serving; regular fruit cocktail in heavy syrup, 90 calories per serving." A reduced-calorie food that does not smell and taste in all respects like the food for which it is offered as a substitute—for instance, canned pears in unsweetened water as compared with canned pears in heavy syrup—must be labeled with information about any differences that exist. If a standardized food is modified so that it no longer complies with the standard, it cannot simply add the words "low calorie" or "reduced calorie" to its name; the food must be labeled "imitation" or be called by another appropriately descriptive name.

For consumers, it means a greater choice of calorie-saving food than ever before. The labels tell the story—and they should be required reading for every smart dieter.

Reading Time: _____
Word Count: 650
Reading Speed: _____

Part 6

Reading Magazines and Journals

Power Reading Facts

In his 1985 book Illiterate America, *author Jonathan Kozol argues that 60 million Americans cannot read. Supporting his assertion are United Nations statistics that rank the United States forty-ninth in literacy among the 158 countries in the UN.*

G eneral-interest magazines are an effective—and enjoyable—way to keep up with the information deluge. Trade journals enable busy executives to stay on top of the latest innovations in their field.

Whether you are reading general magazines for pleasure or special interest publications for profit, the power reading techniques in this chapter can help you get the most from your time.

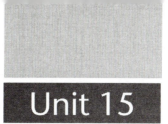

Unit 15

Reading Magazines

In Unit 14, you learned how to make the unique features and structure of a newspaper article work for you. In this lesson, you will learn how power readers do the same thing with magazine articles. You'll see how they capitalize on the structure of a magazine article to read faster and retain more information.

Magazine Features

Like newspaper articles, magazine pieces have very specific layout features and specific methods of organizing material. Titles, graphic displays, typefaces, and headings all offer clues to the contents of the articles. Let's examine them to see how they can work for you.

Titles

Newspaper articles begin with a *headline*; magazine pieces all start off with a *title*. Like a newspaper headline, a magazine title is intended to grab the reader's attention as it suggests the content of the article. Here are some examples:

> *Let's Put Pornography Back in the Closet*
>
> *Cradle-to-Grave Intimacy*
>
> *The Truth About Secondhand Smoke*
>
> *Shopping by TV: Bargains or Bunkum?*
>
> *Those Amazing Infomercials*
>
> *Snapshots Without Tears*
>
> *Stee-rike!*
>
> *China: Economic Superpower of the 21st Century*

Use the title to decide if you want to read the article. If the title does not attract your interest or describe an issue that is important to you, don't waste time; move on!

Graphic Displays

Increasingly, magazines are a visual as well as textual medium. Today's magazines use a variety of visuals to suggest the contents of the article and to attract your eye. Possible visual displays include:

◆ photographs

◆ line drawings

◆ bar, line, or circle graphs

◆ charts

◆ line graphs

◆ cartoons

◆ circle graphs

◆ maps

◆ fine art

◆ diagrams

In most instances, you can get a tremendous amount of information from the graphic display. Reading the *caption* or *label* can often give you nearly as much information as you can get from reading the text itself.

Typefaces

Desk-top publishing and the changing marketplace have both contributed to the changing look of magazines. Now, many magazines use exciting typefaces to vary the way a page looks. This can make it easier to find and read articles. For example, you may see words printed in CAPITAL LETTERS, *italics*, and **boldface**.

Typefaces can also be different sizes, shapes, and colors. In general, the largest, easiest to read typefaces are used for important information. These typefaces help draw your attention to key facts and details in a magazine article. CAPITAL LETTERS and **boldface** are used for words and letters the writer wants to stress. *Italics* are used for the titles of books, record albums, and television shows, for example. *Italics* can also be used to emphasize key words, definitions, and foreign words and phrases. Watch for matching typefaces. Look for words that use all capital letters, boldface, or italics. The information in the same typeface is equally important in the passage.

Don't be slowed down by these visual displays; instead, make them work for you! Follow these steps.

Power Reading Strategy
Making Typefaces Work for You!

1. Move from the largest to the smallest type on the page.

2. Focus on the largest type first. It will present the overview.

3. Move to the next smallest type. It will give more specific details.

4. Pay close attention to information in boldface. It is likely to be very important.

5. Watch for information in italics.

Use your newfound knowledge of typefaces to help speed your way through this music review.

A Guide to Jamaican Rap

Dance-Hall Daze

To delve deeper into the music industrial-strength backbeat, here's a sampling of recent recordings that showcase the genre's urgent and distinctly urban sound.

VARIOUS ARTISTS **Strictly Dancehall** (*Epic/Shang*) The definitive collection, this 1993 disc juxtaposes rising stars like Shabba Ranks and Mad Cobra...alongside older, socially conscious pioneers like Josey Wales. A fine sampler for the uninitiated, and a staple for serious collectors. **A**

SUPER CAT **The Good, the Bad, the Ugly, and the Crazy** (*Columbia*) For hard-hitting fusions of dancehall and rap, Super Cat's performance on the 1993 compilation album NYC Badmen and this new work—recorded with cult hero Nicodemus and musical heirs Junior Cat and Junior Demus—have never been outdone. The beats are as hard as concrete; the vocals, frenetic and furious. **A–**

Headings

Often, magazine editors will insert one or more headings in an article. Just as signposts alert drivers on a busy street, headings signal readers about important parts of the article. Often, just reading the headings and skimming the body of a magazine article will give you all the information that you need. Try it with the following article:

Fat-Free or Fat Chance?

Sin Food: A Fake Revival?

It was just a few years ago that food makers promised that fake fats would create a new world of guilt-free chocolate cake, ice cream, and french fries. They haven't delivered yet, but that hasn't stopped the industry from continuing its crusade....Here's an update from the front:

Salatrim: Nabisco claims it's more like real fat than the others. In other words, the reduced-calorie product re-creates the texture of fat and, as shown in the lab, has a better "mouth feel."

Olestra: Hundreds of millions of dollars later, Procter & Gamble is still trying to get the feds to approve their fake fat, which it hopes to use in fried foods such as potato chips. But it had better hurry— Olestra's patents are running out.

Simplesse: Earlier this year, NutraSweet gave up its version of ice cream called Simple Pleasures. Lousy mouth feel? Perhaps, but the fake stuff is still used in cheese and mayonnaise.

◆ ◆ ◆ ◆

What information did you get from the three headings *Salatrim, Olestra,* and *Simplesse*? The headings, the names of the three artificial fats, give you the handle for the article. They tipped you off about the key points.

Opener

If you still don't have all the information you need after skimming the headline and looking at the graphics, turn to the article's opening paragraph. Recall that the *lead* to a newspaper article uses the five *W's* and *H* to give you all the news at a glance. The opener of a magazine article, in contrast, is designed to grab your attention, not reveal the entire contents of the article. In fact, in many cases, a magazine writer does not want to reveal everything about the article up front. Instead, the writer wants to attract your attention and make you want to read on. Magazine articles often begin with:

◆ provocative dialogue

◆ brief anecdote (story)

◆ startling statement

◆ controversial statement

Reading the opening paragraph of a magazine article will rarely tell you much about the contents of the article. To get the most from your reading time, skim the opening paragraph. Then go on to the body.

Body

Here's where you will find the writer's main ideas. Unlike a newspaper article, the main ideas in a magazine article are *not* arranged from most to least important. Instead, the structure of the body can follow any number of different designs. The most common ways to organize magazine articles are these:

- ◆ problem/solution
- ◆ cause/effect
- ◆ comparison/contrast
- ◆ chronological order
- ◆ spatial order

Let's take a look at each one and see how we can use power reading skills to get the most information in the least time!

Problem/Solution

In these articles, writers state a problem and give one or more solutions. In most cases, the solutions will be arranged from least to most effective. Knowing this, where should you direct your eye? Toward the end of the article! That's where you will find the most important information. Also try to anticipate possible problems and solutions as you read. Active reading strategies work especially well with magazine articles arranged this way.

Here's the opening to a problem/solution article. As you read it, look for the problem and try to predict possible solutions.

> The April 15 deadline for filing federal income tax returns is less than two weeks away, triggering the familiar taxpayer laments about owing too much to the tax collector. The wealthiest taxpayers are as likely to complain as the less well off—and sometimes more so, as the wealthy are more likely to owe the government money, while the poor are more likely to receive a refund. But everyone gripes about high taxes. And not without reason: Taxes are higher; each year the government taxes more money out of our collective pockets. It's no surprise that the tax burden is distributed unfairly. How can the burden be redistributed to be more equitable?

The problem? How to make the tax burden more equitable. The solution? That's what the author will discuss in the rest of the article.

Cause/Effect

In these articles, the writer sets up a situation and describes the results. In most cases, the writer will trace multiple causes and effects, even within a situation that seems relatively simple. Often, writers will telegraph causes and effects with specific signal words. Here are the most common signal words used to show cause and effect:

because	so	so that	then
consequently	thus	since	for
for that reason	as a result	therefore	due to

Power Reading Strategy

When you read cause-and-effect magazine articles, follow these steps.

1. Skim the article to find the specific causes and effects.

2. Look for signal words to find causes and effects.

3. Focus only on those causes and effects that present new facts.

4. Avoid those points that merely restate old information.

Here's a sample cause-and-effect body paragraph. Try the power reading strategy explained above as you read this passage:

> Work is a means of getting money, not in itself a meaningful human activity. Peter Drucker, observing workers in the automobile industry, expresses this idea very succinctly: "For the great majority of automobile workers, the only meaning of the job is in the paycheck, not in anything connected with the work or the product. Work appears as something unnatural, disagreeable, meaningless, and stultifying, devoid of dignity as well as of importance. No wonder that this puts a premium on slovenly work, on slowdowns, and on other tricks to get the same pay with less work. No wonder that this results in an unhappy and discontented worker—because a paycheck is not enough to base one's self-respect on."

Comparison/Contrast

Comparison/contrast articles show how two people, places, things, or ideas are the same (comparison) or different (contrast). Comparison/contrast articles can present their material in two ways:

Introduction

All of topic A

All of topic B

Conclusion

or

Introduction

First aspect of topic A

First aspect of topic B

Second aspect of topic A

Second aspect of topic B

Third aspect of topic A

Third aspect of topic B

Conclusion

As with other types of organization, writers of comparison/contrast articles often use signal words to alert readers to key parts of the argument. Here are the signal words to watch for as you read these types of articles:

Signal Words that Show Contrast

but yet	in contrast	nevertheless
on the other hand	on the contrary	conversely
nonetheless	however	rather

Signal Words that Show Comparison

still	in comparison	similarly
likewise	like	in the same way
at the same time	in the same manner	

Power Reading Strategy

When you read comparison/contrast magazine articles, follow these steps:

1. Skim the article to find out how the writer arranges the argument.

2. Look for signal words to find how the topics are the same and different.

3. Focus on those similarities and differences that present new facts.

4. Avoid those points that merely restate old information.

Here's a sample comparison/contrast body paragraph. Try the power reading strategy explained above as you read this passage.

The Ibos and the Yorubas, prominent African tribes living in Nigeria, are similar in many respects, but one striking difference between them has impressed itself on the minds of visitors more than the similarities between the two cultures. The Ibos have been much influenced by their contacts with Europeans. They have acquired a very deep consciousness of the value of education. Many of them have also become Christians. The Yorubas, likewise, have acquired many Western ways and values. They devote themselves seriously to education, and some, like many of the Ibos, have adopted Christianity. The Ibos, except for the Christians among them, practice polygamy. The Yorubas who have not been converted to Christianity also practice polygamy. The Christians among them do not. What separates the two Nigerian tribes decisively in the mind of outsiders, however, is a wide difference in the attitude of the two peoples toward the supernatural. Belief in supernatural powers does not play an important part in the life of the Ibo tribesman. On the other hand, the Yoruba man and woman find life governed to a large extent by a real belief in the existence of spirits and supernatural powers which are very close and must be considered in daily life. Belief in such spirits is obvious in the stories, art, and customs that visitors become aware of.

Chronological Order

An article arranged in chronological order presents events in the order of time, from the most distant to the most recent events. This arrangement allows writers to unfold events gradually and to build to a climax. As a result, this arrangement is most often used in *narrative* writing, writing that tells a story. For example, you will find chronological order in an anecdote.

Passages arranged in chronological order are difficult for speed readers, because each of the details is weighted equally. You cannot skim easily, because there is too great a risk of missing a key event. You do not know which details will be important for complete understanding of the article.

You can, however, check for words that signal key points or transitions in events. Words and phrases to locate include:

first	next	when
second	then	during
third	later	in the future
fourth	so	now
today	since	at that moment
yesterday	soon	earlier
after	last	long ago
while	finally	before

Spatial Order

In this method, the writer arranges all the events from a reference point. Events can be arranged from top to bottom, bottom to top, inside to outside, outside to inside, point A to point B, and so on. This method is used most often for descriptive writing, such as travelogues and fashion shows.

To read these articles quickly and accurately, find the words that indicate that the action is moving from one location to another. Such words include:

over	under	here
there	beside	near

Here's an example. As you read the excerpt, try to see how the writer has arranged the details.

Nameless, Tennessee, was a town of maybe ninety people if you pushed it, a dozen houses along the road, a couple of barns, same number of churches, a general merchandise store selling Fire Chief gasoline, and a community center with a lighted volleyball court. Behind the center was an open-roof, rusting metal privy with PAINT ME on the door, in the hollow of a nearby oak lay a full pint of Jack Daniels Black Label. The odor of coal smoke drifted from the houses.

(The writer followed the arrangement of stores on the main street)

◆   ◆   ◆   ◆

How much time should it take you to read the average general-interest magazine article? No more than 2 *minutes*! How can you get the most from a magazine article—*fast*? Follow these steps:

Power Reading Strategy

1. Read the title.

2. Explore the graphic displays, especially the captions and labels.

3. Focus on the largest type features. See what they have to say.

4. Skim the first two or three paragraphs.

5. Skim the first sentence of each additional paragraph. This will show you how the author develops the ideas.

6. Skim the final paragraph.

But keep in kind that power reading is not only reading faster, it's knowing how to spend your valuable reading time. If a magazine article doesn't interest you, don't read it. Determine where your time is best spent. If you're stuck on line at the supermarket or the bank, you are much better off reading a magazine article of marginal interest than waiting for your blood pressure to rise. Remember: Reading *any* article will increase your speed and comprehension. Even if it is an article that normally would not interest you, if you have nothing else to do, read it! But if you are fortunate enough to have a choice of reading materials, select the ones that will teach you the most or entertain you the best.

Exercise

Read each of the following passages from various magazine articles. Then identify the structure of each. To help you find the structure, look for signal words.

1.   Mr. Mom

Ruben Garcia wishes that, just once, someone would compliment him on his newly polished floor, his freshly ironed shirts, and his tasty pot roast. One of an increasing number of stay-at-home dads, Garcia says he wants a little respect. He cooks, cleans, and carpools for this three children full time with no complaints—and receives little or no recognition for a hard day's work....

Garcia, 39, a former airline mechanic, was injured on the job in 1985, and has been unable to find similar work. With his wife working as a secretary, he has become a stay-at-home dad.

"I had to adjust to a new way of thinking," he says. "I had to rearrange my priorities. I was forced to become a mother and a father. By staying at home, I have learned what most men don't learn in a lifetime. When a child first learns to walk, talk, count, or dress himself or herself, it's a joyful thing. And when you're away from home all day, you miss it."

Structure_____

2.   Unsafe Ingredients

The real "cotton tragedy"—over and above the maimed and the dead—was that it took so long to act in what was an open-and-shut case. The answers are seldom so clear-cut with suspected ingredients: hexachlorophene was a "miracle ingredient" until it was banned about ten years after its safety was questioned; the vinyl chloride propellant in aerosols was considered just a harmless inert gas until very recently.

Structure_____

3.   Sharks

Described as "a swimming, eating, and reproducing machine without peer," the shark is considered an evolutionary success story, having changed little in over 60 million years. Sharks are models of efficiency with their boneless skeletons, simple brains and generalized nervous systems, and simple internal structures. Their hydrodynamically designed shapes, razor-sharp replacement teeth, powerful jaws, and voracious appetites make them excellent marauders. Through scavenging and predation, the 250 species of sharks perform a valuable service in maintaining the ecological balance of the oceans. Their well-developed sensory systems enable them to detect extreme dilutions of blood in water, low frequency sounds of splashing made by fish in distress, and movements and contrast in water.

Structure_____

4. Old October

October is the richest of seasons; the fields are cut, the granaries are full, the bins are loaded to the brim with fatness, and from the cider press the rich brown oozings of the York Imperials run. The bee bares to the belly of the yellowed grape, the fly gets old and fat and blue, he buzzes loud, crawls slow, creeps heavily to death on sill and ceiling, the sun goes down in blood across the bronzed and mown fields of October.

Structure_____

5. Anyone for Whale Meat?

The Inuit (Eskimos) eat more fat than any other people in the world, but heart disease (often caused by a fatty diet) is rare among them. The reason? Eskimos eat a lot of fish, whale, and seal. These foods are high in unsaturated fats, which do not lead to heart disease. The typical American diet of butter, red meat, and eggs is rich in saturated fats, the "bad" fats that can cause heart attacks.

Structure_____

6. How Much Are You Worth?

Have you tried filling out a net worth statement as a means of keeping tabs on yourself and your family possessions? Such a record provides a good overall picture and can be prepared in an hour or less. If you do it annually, you can see quickly whether you are getting ahead financially or falling behind and, in either case, how fast.

An accurate net worth statement can serve as a point of departure for the year ahead. If you're not making as much progress financially as you had expected, you can decide whether to stay on course or to change direction for the coming year.

Where are you going to find a net worth form that will meet your needs? Try your county Cooperative Extension Service office. Or ask at your bank. Better yet, perhaps you can make one yourself to meet your family's needs. All you do is list your assets, list your obligations, and subtract the debts from the assets. Hopefully the plus side of the ledger will get larger each year and the minus side smaller. But there may be good reasons why you'll fall behind sometimes, such as when you buy a new home or when other expenses are heavier than usual.

Structure_____

7. The Positive Woman

The first requirement for the acquisition of power by the Positive Woman is to understand the differences between men and women. Your outlook on life, your faith, your behavior, and your potential for fulfillment are all determined by the parameters of your original premise. The Positive Woman starts with the assumption that the world is her oyster. She rejoices in the creative capability within her body and the power potential of her mind and spirit. She understands that men and women are different, and that these very differences provide the key to her success as a person and her fulfillment as a woman.

Structure_____

Answers

1. comparison/contrast
2. problem/solution
3. cause/effect
4. spatial order
5. comparison/contrast
6. problem/solution
7. comparison/contrast

Exercise

Read the following magazine article as quickly as you can. Identify the structure and use it to help you in your reading. Use the other techniques you learned as well. Time yourself to calculate your reading speed.

Catchin' Some Rays

This year Americans will spend about $50 million in search of a look that most won't acquire: the even, golden tan that looks super-rich, lasts for months, and never peels or wrinkles.

When you take your place in the sun this summer, your goal probably will be "increased formation of melanin pigment by specialized cells in the skin's basal layer and upward migration of the melanin to the external surface." In other words, you want a tan.

What you may get instead is inflammation and fluid infiltration, which translates, of course, to burning and blistering. You may also increase your risk of getting skin cancer.

Unless you use good judgment and skin protection, you could join the majority of sunbathers whose few days of "vacation tan" will be paid for by uncomfortable skin that soon peels. Or you may join the group that spends several days of vacation time recovering from the mistakes of the first couple of days.

But whether your hours in the sun are out of luxury or necessity, whether you're trying to obtain a tan or just working or playing outdoors, it will pay you to learn more about suntans.

Who Needs Protection?

The effects of sunlight on a person's skin vary with the amount of ultraviolet light that an individual can take. Some people under ordinary circumstances (short exposures) seem to tan without burning; others burn first, then tan; and others burn, peel, burn again, and never tan. So who needs protection? Everyone!

The amount of sun you can take depends largely on the thickness of your skin and to a lesser extent on pigmentation. Whichever group you're in, however, too much sunlight can yield a burn. Therefore, there's no reason for anyone to sunbathe without the protection of a sunscreen, hat, and light clothing.

High-risk groups for concentrated exposures to the sun, especially on hot days, are old people and people with light skin. Both are more easily susceptible to burning, and the elderly are less able to cope with any resulting infection or trauma.

Another situation that could predispose you to redness and pigmented spots is the use of fragrances—aftershaves, cologne, and so on—directly on the skin before bathing. These may contain bergapten, a chemical capable of reacting with the sunlight to produce a phototoxic reaction in the skin.

The Illusive Shortcut

If you're on your once-a-year vacation and it's your only time to soak up some sun, or if you've planned a long weekend at the beach, these warnings are probably falling on deaf ears. The only precaution you're likely to take is extensive use of a "suntan" product, and if you think you're burning (and when you begin to see some signs or feel uncomfortable, then you *are*), you might be persuaded to throw on a loose-fitting shirt and maybe a hat.

If you do use a good suntan preparation, you should be able to stay out all day without burning. So how come you often burn anyway? Perhaps you forgot that swimming, perspiration, or contact with towels, clothing, or sand all remove some of the preparation you have so carefully applied; reapplication in all of these situations is essential.

Or it may be that the product you used was not applied evenly or simply didn't form the kind of overall protective barrier needed; that is, some may seem to lie along the skin in tiny beads, allowing ultraviolet light to penetrate between them. Creams and lotions often do the best job of even distribution and protection.

One point to remember is that no product makes you tan *faster* than you would with no such protection; the aim of such a product is solely to help you stay outside a little longer without burning. (And some preparations, such as baby oil, only keep you greased up and more comfortable while you fry about as fast as you would with nothing on your skin.) A good rule of thumb is to use a sunscreen with an SPF (protection index) of at least a 20. Reapply the sunscreen often, especially if you have gone into the ocean or a pool or if you have been perspiring heavily. Try to avoid being in the sun between the hours of 11:00 and 2:00, when the sun's rays are strongest.

A good skin preparation can help you. But it can't take the place of good judgment.

What Sort of Protection?

There's quite a range of protection available—from nothing but an emollient such as baby oil to almost total blockout as offered by a generous application of zinc oxide (that white blob you often see slathered on a lifeguard's nose), or just plain old calamine lotion (which is also derived from zinc) mixed with cold cream. Between these extremes is the ever-increasing variety of creams, lotions, clear liquids, butters, gels, and aerosol foams from which most sunbathers choose.

Although we offer here some words of advice for those who have been less than successful in the game of suntanning and protection, no one would presume to argue with success. If you've found a method and a product that works well for you, stick with it.

But remember that tanning *always* leaves irrevocable signs of premature aging of the skin. Even if you develop the best tan of your life, with no burning or discomfort, at some point—when will vary with each person—your skin will begin to look leathery, thick, and wrinkled, no matter how soft to the touch.

The best advice is not to push your luck. Even small amounts of sun speed up the aging process of the skin. So you're well advised to quit tanning when you're ahead, *before* you detect burning. Even careful sunbathing, year after year, will bring out the age signs quickly, since the effects of the sun are both insidious and cumulative. This goes for *all* ages.

In Spite of Everything...

If you *do* sunburn:

1. If the burn is severe, see a doctor. Sunburn can make you very sick with chills, fever, and even delirium. Also, bad blisters always need the attention of a physician, because of the danger of infection.

2. In mild cases where the skin turns red, dust the area with talcum powder.

3. For moderately bad burns where the skin is red and slightly swollen, apply wet dressings of gauze dipped in a solution of

baking soda and cornstarch—1 tablespoon of each to 2 quarts of cool water; or use cool milk or water in an emergency.

Best Bet

To make sure you can fully enjoy time in the sun without setting yourself up for early wrinkles and damaged, peeling skin, start off gradually, use the protection best suited for your activity, and don't shorten your overall time in the sun by trying to soak it all up in the first few days.

Reading Time: _____
Word Count: 1100
Reading Speed: _____

Specialized and Technical Materials

In some ways, certain books are more powerful by far than any battle.
                                                    —*Henry A. Wallace*

W hat's a specialized or technical publication? It's the government paper you read to prepare for a meeting, the annual reports you study for investment purposes, the position paper you have to condense and fax to your colleagues in another country. It's the lab report, the profit-and-loss statement, and the business newsletter on technology and innovation. It's an article on alternative energy projects, a report on wireless services on data networks, a booklet on the Maglev. It's any specialized material aimed at people with technical or professional concerns.

Special Materials Need Special Techniques

Specialized and technical materials demand special reading techniques. Why? Specialized materials differ in content from everyday reading. Unlike newspaper and magazine articles, these materials are densely packed with facts, details, and examples. They are often filled with jargon—technical terms—as well. This difference in style requires a difference in reading method. Try this unique power reading method.

Skim, Mark, Read, Reread

This powerful reading method can shave precious minutes from your reading time. Here's how it's done:

Skim to Preview the Content

Recall that when you skim an article you read it at your fastest possible speed, letting your eyes glance over key words, numbers, and graphics. Skimming means that you read groups of words, numbers of lines, and chunks of text rather than individual words, phrases, and lines. When you skim technical articles, focus on these parts:

title

author

headings

footnotes or endnotes

subheads

bibliography or Works Cited page

photographs

charts

graphs

drawings

Also pay attention to any material that is indented, numbered, or set off in any way. Try it with the excerpt below from a technical article. Then answer the questions that follow.

Mutual Funds

by Melinda Worthsworth, Certified Financial Planner

Ranking Systems

When investing in mutual funds, focus on fund performance over three to five years. Shorter periods aren't meaningful, and longer periods may include results earned when the fund had different investment objectives or was managed by different fund managers. Rank funds against other funds with similar investment objectives, and be sure that any ranking system includes a measure of the risk each fund incurs in relation to its returns. Avoid relying on ranking systems that are overly complex or that you don't understand.[1]

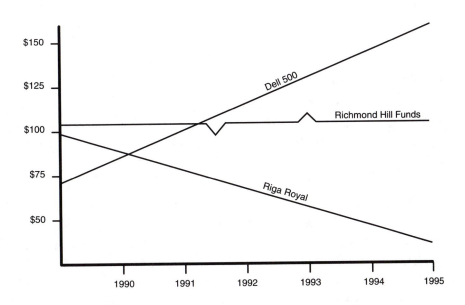

Exercise

1. What did you learn from the title?

_____

2. What can you infer from skimming the author's name?

_____

3. What information did you get from the subheading?

_____

4. What does the footnote indication suggest?

_____

5. Did you find the chart helpful? Why or why not?

_____

Answers

1. The article will be about buying mutual funds.

2. The Certified Financial Planner designation suggests that she is probably well qualified to write about investing.

3. The following passage will be about methods used to rank mutual funds.

4. It suggests that the author has done research on this topic and so consulted other sources.

5. Yes, because it reveals a great deal of information in a brief space.

Mark Key Places in the Text

As you skim, take a few seconds to mark key places in the text. There are several different ways that you can do this: underlining, highlighting, writing tick marks, stars, or dashes in the margin. Many people find that using their pencil as both a tracer and a writing tool works well; other prefer to use a yellow or pink highlighter. We recommend that you try out different methods until you find the one that gives you the greatest speed coupled with the greatest comprehension and accuracy.

Mark **only** key words and phrases. Omit prepositions (over, under, below, in, to, from, by, etc.) conjunctions (and, but, or, for, nor, so, yet, etc.), articles (a, an, the), and unnecessary adjectives and adverbs. Concentrate on nouns and verbs—the meat of the sentence. You are better off marking too little than too much text. Remember: This is intended to be a fast process. Keep your marking system simple and avoid complex codes and symbols. If you take too much time marking the text, you will lose both meaning and speed, defeating your purpose.

No matter which system you use, you should mark the following places in the text:

topic sentences

key words

important phrases

crucial concepts

Try marking the following excerpt from a technical article on high blood cholesterol.

How to Lower Your High Blood Cholesterol

Saturated fats raise your cholesterol level more than anything else in your diet. Dietary cholesterol also raises blood cholesterol levels. Instead of eating foods rich in saturated fat and cholesterol, try more breads, cereals, and other foods high in complex carbohydrates as well as more fruits and vegetables. Using unsaturated fats in place of saturated fats can also help lower your blood cholesterol.

There are two kinds of unsaturated fat: polyunsaturated and monounsaturated. You should substitute both of these for saturated fat in your diet. Polyunsaturated fats are found primarily in plant products—including safflower, sunflower, corn, soybean, and cottonseed oils; nuts; and seeds—and in fattening dishes. Major vegetable oil sources of monounsaturated fats are primarily olive oil and canola oil.

Cholesterol is found only in foods of animal origin, both high-fat foods (like hot dogs and cheddar cheese) and low-fat foods (like liver and other organ meats). And the amount of cholesterol in these foods varies. A daily intake of less than 300mg is recommended. A 3-ounce piece of meat, fish, or poultry has 60–90mg of cholesterol; one egg yoke contains about 270mg; and a 3-ounce serving of liver has about 390mg of cholesterol.

Answers

Here are some places you should have noted:

title: How to Lower Your High Blood Cholesterol

topic sentence: Saturated fats raise your cholesterol level more than anything else in your diet.

Key words and phrases:

◆ try more breads, cereals, and other foods high in complex carbohydrates

◆ polyunsaturated and monounsaturated fats

◆ cholesterol is found only in foods of animal origin

Read the Article Quickly

Now it's time to read a technical article at your fastest speed. Try to move as quickly as you can through the article. Because you have already skimmed and marked the text, you should be able to read quite fast. Your familiarity with the text will help you read much more quickly than you imagine.

Pull together everything you have learned so far in this lesson by reading skimming, marking, and reading the following specialized article. Time yourself to calculate your reading speed.

The Future of Maglev

One key factor in transportation is not how fast you get from one station to another, but how fast you reach your destination. Airplanes have a disadvantage because of the need to go to airports or town centers to begin or end the trip. Maglev—magnetically levitated vehicles—will take you to the town center and so intermodally it connects the population centers. There is no reason that it couldn't connect into existing rails, buses, and so forth. Because Maglev is a new system it could be put in anywhere. Planners are not constrained to the existing transportation system.

Maglev makes sense because it has no moving parts and it is very reliable. One analogy is that Maglev stands to the steel rail in the same way that the laser printer stands to the typewriter.

Maglev is more than speed; it many cases, it makes sense even for low-speed operations. When it comes to short distances such as New York City to Washington, D.C., for example, the airplane is extremely inefficient, depends on an expensive infrastructure, runs up high fuel costs, and creates heavy pollution. One Maglev will have about ten times the capacity of a typical highway.

Unfortunately, while the technology exists, it is too expensive at this time to be feasible. However, both Germany and Japan have successfully used magnetically levitated vehicles for transport. The German and Japanese experiences represent both the good and the bad news for the American Maglev technology. The fact that it exists helps, because it is something that we can point to and say, "It's not science fiction, it's fact." That's the good news. The bad news is that the number of potential passengers in the German and Japanese systems is so high they don't have to worry about the same economies Americans must consider.

As a result, both the German and Japanese have built a system that is far more expensive than what the American market can justify. And so, Americans must improve the technology in such a way as to drive the price down.

To meet this goal, American engineers took the German concept and used superconducting magnets to increase the air gap from $3/8$ inch to 2 inches. It turns out that this saves weight because when you have a 2-inch air gap, the guideway structure does not have to be aligned as precisely as when the gap is $3/8$ inch. The only way to maintain such precise alignment is if the guide way is massive and heavy, which translates into higher cost.

Many experts believe that American Maglev systems could be built at considerably less cost than German Maglev systems. Already New York State has announced ambitious plans to establish Maglev systems. Estimates claim the systems could be operational by 2005.

Reading Time: _____
Word Count: 450
Reading Speed: _____

Reread

You're not done quite yet! Now it's time to take a few minutes to go back over the text. Since specialized articles tend to be highly technical, it's worth the extra time to return to the text and reread key passages. Unless you had a serious problem with comprehension, you should be able to reread very quickly. Very quickly! Follow these steps:

1. Reread the topic sentences in each paragraph.

2. Reread highlighted passages.

3. Reread the closing sentences.

Take a few minutes to reread the Maglev article. To test your comprehension, you may wish to summarize the article briefly as well. When you finish rereading, look up from the text. Take a moment to think about what you have read. Then compose a brief summary in your mind. Keep your summary short—no more than a sentence or two.

Exercise

Try the entire process with the following special-interest article on the environment. Remember to follow these four steps:

1. Skim

2. Mark

3. Read

4. Reread

Don't forget to time yourself. Go for the burn—but don't sacrifice comprehension. Specialized and technical articles call for particular attention to understanding.

Linking Economic and Environmental Goals

Environmental problems are capturing worldwide attention at a time of intensifying global economic competition. As a result, society faces the need to understand and address links between environmental policies and those of trade, technology, and competitiveness. Technology and policies that promote technological innovation and efficiency are key to resolving many pressing environmental problems, to boosting the long-term export potential of U.S. environmental firms, and to making it less costly for firms to comply with environmental regulations.

Industry is increasingly affected by changing competitive realities shaped by environmental expectations of its customers and the societies in which it operates. This article focuses on the competitive challenges and opportunities for two kinds of American industries that are affected by environmental regulations: (1) environmental technology and service firms; (2) manufacturing firms in general that are responding to requirements for reducing pollution.

In the first case, U.S. environmental firms may be able to benefit from unprecedented opportunities to expand into new markets likely to develop in the years ahead as more countries establish or tighten environmental standards. U.S. firms currently are competitive in most environmental sectors but face intensifying competition from firms in Europe, Japan, and some newly industrialized countries. Some predict huge worldwide markets for environmental technologies and services—perhaps exceeding $300 billion per year by the end of the decade. Most of this demand will be filled locally. However, trade is still sizable, and prospects for increasing U.S. exports are probably greatest for relatively sophisticated equipment and services. While the growth in U.S. jobs related to such an increase may be modest, many of these jobs will be high-wage technical or engineering jobs.

As for U.S. manufacturing firms, the environmental regulations that benefit society as a whole represent a competitive challenge. While pollution control is not a top-ranking factor affecting competitiveness, it does add to manufacturing costs. U.S. manufacturers have faced stiff competition from able foreign competitors in the last decade, and differences in pollution control compliance costs between the United States and other nations have the potential to affect relative competitive positions. Compliance costs incurred by U.S. manufacturers for pollution control are among the highest in the world, apparently exceeding those in Japan and many European nations. Moreover, some countries provide their companies with greater financial and technical help in complying with pollution abatement requirements.

A major economic and environmental opportunity for the future will be to integrate environmental concerns into the next generation of manufacturing technologies. Cleaner, more cost-effective production technologies could help U.S. manufacturers reduce compliance costs while still meeting U.S. environmental standards, which are likely to remain the toughest in the world. Such technologies could also be the key to maintaining a highly competitive environmental industry with the strong export potential needed to generate jobs for American workers.

Cleaner production technologies are also critical for progress toward the goal of sustainable development—an overriding global need for the long term. More cost effective than conventional controls alone, they have the potential to ease conflicts between economic and environmental goals.

Debate is underway about the U.S. government's role in both promoting development and trade in environmental technology and in helping U.S. firms meet environmental standards with greater cost effectiveness. Governmental regulations both create markets for environmental technologies and the compliance conditions faced by industry. Another issue is how to ensure that the federal government's sizable research and development budget for environmentally preferable technologies produces commercial as well as environmental benefits for U.S. society. Other policy areas, including manufacturing research and development, industrial extension, and export promotion, also could affect development, diffusion, and trade in environmental technologies.

Congress has more than thirty policy options to consider. Among them:

◆ devise a strategy to promote development and widespread domestic diffusion of environmentally preferable technologies

◆ create mechanisms to integrate environmental objectives into government support for manufacturing industry R&D

◆ develop regulatory approaches that allow firms that are first-rate environmental performers more choice in how they meet environmental requirements

◆ use export promotion and development assistance programs to encourage export of environmentally and developmentally sound U.S. technologies

◆ work toward agreements that help other nations achieve environmental goals, lessen the likelihood of adverse competitive impact for U.S. firms and workers, and expand opportunities for U.S. environmental firms abroad

Reading Time: _____

Word Count: 850

Reading Speed: _____

Part 7

Reading Textbooks

People…automatically believe in books. This is strange but it is so. Messages come from behind the controlled and censored areas of the world and they do not ask for radios, for papers and pamphlets. They invariably ask for books. They believe in books when they believe nothing else.

—John Steinbeck

John Steinbeck, winner of the 1963 Nobel Prize for Literature, recognized that books convey an authority that no other media can command. As symbols of academia, textbooks occupy a special niche. They're also the type of book we use most often to study specific subjects. We realize that textbooks contains vast tracts of knowledge in every field—so they pack a big wallop in a relatively small space. In the following unit, you'll learn the power reading method for getting the information you need from textbooks—*fast!*

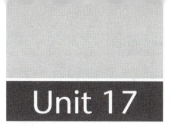

Unit 17

Studying and Retaining Information

S tudying is *not* the same as reading. When you read e-mail, faxes, letters, memos, and articles, you normally skim to extract only the meat of the text. After you read the communication, you act on it. For example, when you receive e-mail, you follow these steps:

1. Power read the message

2. Act on the information

3. Move on to the next task

When you study, in contrast, you must digest and retain facts. You're not taking action; rather, you're memorizing information. You follow these steps:

1. Preview

2. Read

3. Review

Let's take a look at each step in detail.

1. Preview

As you preview the text, look specifically at the:

◆ title of the textbook

◆ table of contents

Since your purpose is to learn the facts in the text, focus on the facts, not the layout of the book. After you preview the text itself, focus on these areas:

◆ subheads

◆ pictures

◆ photographs

◆ graphs

◆ abstracts

◆ figures

◆ charts and tables

◆ other graphic organizers

◆ glossaries

Preview the text below. Then do the exercise that follows to analyze what you learned from your preview.

American State Offices in Europe: Activities and Connections

Abstract

The emergence of global economic competition, especially from Europe and Asia, has drawn many states—as well as cities, counties, and port authorities—into the international arena, where they have sought to promote state and local exports, attract investment, and encourage tourism. One vehicle for carrying out these activities has been to open state offices in Europe, Asia, Latin America, and elsewhere. Here, we focus on state offices in Europe.

Locations

Most of the state offices are clustered in a few major cities: thirteen in Brussels, eleven in Frankfurt, and two in Düsseldorf (see Table 1). European cities having only one American state office include Amsterdam, Berlin, Hanover, Paris, Rijsbergen, Warsaw, and Budapest. In addition, nine states have port authority offices, of which four are located in Belgium.

Table 1
State Offices in Europe

State	Office Location
Alabama	Hannover
Arkansas	Brussels
California	London, Frankfurt
Colorado	Brussels
Connecticut	Frankfurt
Florida	London, Frankfurt
Georgia	Brussels
Illinois	Brussels, Warsaw, Budapest
Indiana	Amsterdam
Iowa	Frankfurt
Kansas	Brussels
Kentucky	Brussels
Louisiana	Rijsbergen
Maryland	Brussels
Massachusetts	Berlin
Michigan	Brussels
Mississippi	Frankfurt
Missouri	Düsseldorf
New York	London, Frankfurt
North Carolina	Düsseldorf
Ohio	Brussels
Oklahoma	Frankfurt
Pennsylvania	Frankfurt, Brussels
Puerto Rico	Brussels
South Carolina	Frankfurt
Texas	Frankfurt
Utah	Waterloo
Virginia	Brussels
Washington	Paris

Territories Covered by State Offices

Most state offices cannot serve their full territory adequately, so they focus on their immediate surroundings. The prime target of state efforts is Germany, followed closely by Britain and France. Together, these three countries consume over half the state efforts in Europe. This focus does not directly correlate with office locations, due to the large number of offices in Brussels and only one in France. Five percent of state efforts are directed toward Eastern Europe, in part because of the difficulties of doing business there (see Table 2).

Table 2
Regions Covered by State Offices
(Percent of Effort per Region)

Regions	Percent
Germany	27.3
United Kingdom	17.2
France	16.2
Benelux	13.1
Italy and Spain	8.1
Scandinavia	8.1
Eastern Europe	5.0
Other	5.0

In early 1995, a cable was sent to overseas commercial posts, stating, in part:

There is a critical need to update the FTI (Foreign Trader Index)... The FTI is badly out of date. Now that many overseas posts have new CIMS Plus, or will shortly get it, the means are available to begin the process. (As of December 1, 1994, only six posts have been advised that they will not meet the target date.)

Figure 1

State Sources of Information
on European Importers

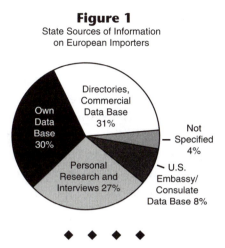

◆ ◆ ◆ ◆

Exercise

Complete the following table to summarize what you have learned.

Part of the Text	Information Provided
Title _____
Abstract_____
Table 1_____
Subheads_____
Table 2_____
Figure 1 _____

Answers

Part of the Text	Information Provided
Title	contents of the chapter
Abstract	summary of the chapter
Table 1	location of state offices in Europe
Subheads	contents of each section
Table 2	regions covered by state offices
Figure 1	state sources of information on European importers

2. Read

Before you read, decide on your *purpose*. Are you reading to learn the material in the text for a minor quiz? Or are you reading the text to extract important points for a major test? Perhaps you are reading the text to learn information that you will need for your career. Match your reading style to your purpose. For example, if you are reading for a quiz, you will need to recall facts for a short period of time. As a result, you can read more quickly than if you want to recall facts to use in your life or your job. In that case, you will want to focus on comprehension rather than on speed. Use these bar graphs as a guideline:

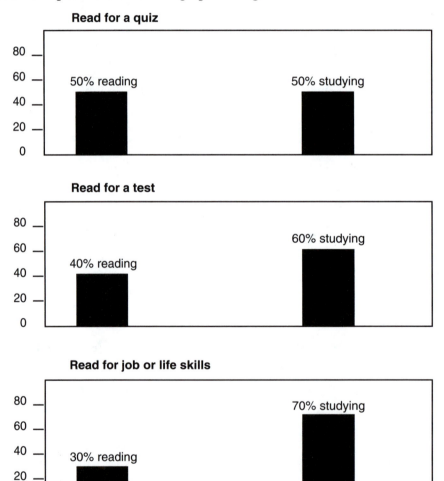

Read for a quiz

80	
60	50% reading 50% studying
40	
20	
0	

Read for a test

80	
60	60% studying
40	40% reading
20	
0	

Read for job or life skills

80	70% studying
60	
40	30% reading
20	
0	

Analyze your purpose and match your reading style accordingly.

No matter what your purpose, read the text at your fastest—but most comfortable—rate. Try to move as quickly as you can, but don't sacrifice comprehension. Remember: you're reading a textbook!

As you read, mark key places in the text. Don't overlook confusing parts! If you reach a sentence, paragraph, or page that you don't understand, put a mark in the margin. This might be a crucial point—or it might be nothing.

Scan for information that pertains the to test. Look for facts that you think you will have to know. Try this method with the following passage:

Naturalization: How to Become an American Citizen

(1) First, every applicant for naturalization must demonstrate an understanding of the English language, including the ability to read, write, and speak words in ordinary usage of the English language (persons physically unable to do so and persons who, on the date of their examinations, are over fifty years of age and have been lawful permanent residents of the United States for twenty years or more are exempt);

(2) Next, have been a person of good moral character, attached to the principles of the Constitution, as well as disposed to the good order and happiness of the United States for five years just before filing the petition or for whatever other period of residence is required in the particular case and continues to be such a person until admitted to citizenship;

(3) Finally, demonstrate a knowledge and understanding of the fundamentals of the history, and the principles and form of government, of the United States.

(4) Later, at the preliminary hearing, the applicant may be represented by a lawyer or social service agency. There is a thirty-day wait. If action is favorable, there is a final hearing before a judge, who administers the oath of allegiance.

◆ ◆ ◆ ◆

Exercise

1. The most important fact in the first paragraph is:

_____

2. What are you likely to be asked about the second paragraph?

_____

3. What is the key detail in the third paragraph?

_____

4. Make up a test question about the information in the fourth paragraph.

_____

Answers

1. Applicants must have a working understanding of English.

2. Applicants must have a good moral character and fulfill the residency requirement.

3. Applicants must know and understand U.S. history and government.

4. What happens if the applicant is naturalized?

3. Review

As you review, spend most of your time looking back over the key parts of the text. Also look back to any places that you found confusing. Don't spend a lot of time here! Take a few seconds to decide if the point is important. If it is, figure it out. If it's not, move right on.

When you have finished your review, briefly summarize what you read. Be sure to state your summary in your own words. It should be no more than two to three lines long.

Read the following speech. Then summarize the speech on the lines provided.

Tell General Howard I know his heart. What he told me before I have in my heart. I am tired of fighting. Our chiefs are killed. Looking Glass is dead. The old men are all killed. It is the young men who say yes or no. He who led the young men is dead. It is cold and we have no blankets. The little children are freezing to death. My people, some of them, have run away to the hills and have no blankets, no food; no one knows where they are, perhaps freezing to death. I want time to look for my children and see how many of them I can find. Maybe I shall find them among the dead. Hear me, my chiefs, I am tired; my heart is sick and sad. From where the sun now stands, I will fight no more forever.

Summary

_____

_____

_____

_____

Answer

The wording of your summary will naturally be different from ours, but the summary should nonetheless contain all the information as this one.

> We will not fight anymore because our leaders and old men have been killed, our children are freezing to death, and I am sick at heart. I want to find my children and see how many I can save.

To get the most from reading a textbook, you must combine speed with comprehension. Use the power reading techniques you have learned on the following two exercises, excerpts from textbooks. Be sure to preview, read, and review. Time yourself to calculate your reading speed.

Understanding Your Credit History

Abstract

Credit bureaus do not make credit decisions: all they do is supply information on which credit granters make their own decisions. What you need to know, therefore, is what information is in your credit record and what you can do if that information is incorrect.

What Is in Your Credit History

There are three basic kinds of information in your credit history:

1. Factual information you have supplied on credit applications: your name and your spouse's (on a joint application), current and former addresses, Social Security number, and employment history.

2. A credit "profile" based on reports from creditors, summarizing your credit history; the accounts you have, their opening dates, the last purchase, amount owed, amount past due, and your usual manner of payment (within 30 days, 30 to 60 days, etc.).

3. Data from public records related in any way to credit, such as bankruptcies, court judgments, and dispositions of lawsuits.

What Is Not in Your Credit History

Contrary to what you may have heard, what is usually not in your credit record are comments from neighbors, friends, and associates about your character, your reputation, and your lifestyle. Such investigative reports are sometimes obtained by insurance companies if you apply for a sizable policy, but you must be notified in writing if a company orders such a report. Credit bureaus do not employ outside investigators and do not furnish investigative reports.

If Your Credit Record Is Incorrect

Inaccurate information has been known to creep into credit files. Perhaps someone with a name similar to yours fails to pay some bills. Perhaps someone fraudulently uses your account and runs up charges. Perhaps you had a legitimate dispute with a merchant over a bill; the dispute has been settled but that fact has not been reported. What can you do? Under the federal Fair Credit Reporting Act you have the right to know what is in your credit file. If you have been turned down for credit within the last 30 days (you must be told if you've been denied credit because of a credit report), you cannot be charged a fee to review this file. If you find an error in your file, you can request an investigation.

Reading Time: _____
Word Count: 390
Reading Speed: _____

Cable Companies Board the Fiber-Optic Highway

Using Fiber Optics

In an effort to position itself in the interactive multimedia industry, a number of major industries around the country are installing high-speed, high-capacity, digital-ready fiber-optic networks. Under fiber optics, companies can send huge amounts of data, voice, or image communications over a single line with much higher signal quality than standard coaxial cables could provide. Other advantages of fiber-optic cables include a much greater band width capability than coaxial cables provide, which means that more data can be sent over less wire, and the elimination of the need for signal amplification, which means that less equipment is needed to transmit a signal. Fiber optics are useful in many industries, but the cable television companies have been among the quickest to seize this technology.

"We are entering a new era of menu-driven services that will give subscribers complete choice and instantaneous access to a virtually unlimited range of television, telecommunications, entertainment, and data services," said Charles Dolan, the Chairman of Cablevision, the fourth largest cable operator in the country and Long Island's ninth largest public company.

Wide Variety of Services

In America, most cable operators are staying competitive by replacing old cable networks with fiber-optical networks, with which they can offer services including video conferencing, picture phones, digital-quality audio transmissions, alternative phone services, high-speed computer interconnections, and hundreds of television channels.

Currently, Cablevision has 550 sheath miles of optical fiber, which consists of thin and transparent plastic or glass strands coated with protective material that guide light through their repeated internal reflections from their surfaces. Nonetheless, to achieve the standards and services they desire, many cable companies are finding that they have to install sophisticated digital compression, switching, and storage systems.

Additional Uses

Other media services are seeking additional uses for fiber-optic technology. Media Services, Inc., for example, has the capacity to link more than forty business customers to long distance carriers through a microwave tower on top of the World Trade Center. Fibernet, Inc., a Queens, New York–based cable company, last year connected business telephone users in thirty-two buildings in Rochester, New York, to long-distance carriers over the fiber-optic network. The company then expanded to Albany, New York, and Cincinnati, Ohio, to provide its services as a competitive access provider (CAP).

Using a Dedicated Synchronous Optical Network (SONET), a growing body of standards that define all aspects of transporting and managing digital traffic over a fiber-optic network, other firms can enable researchers to link computers across the country, transmit x-rays from hospital to hospital, and participate in teleconferences, courses, and lectures.

Reading Time: _____

Word Count: 460

Reading Speed: _____

Part 8

Reading for Pleasure

Books rule the world, or at least those nations which have a written language; the others do not count.

—Voltaire

Can you apply the power reading techniques you learned in previous lessons to pleasure reading? Yes! These techniques can help you minimize your reading time and maximize your comprehension. In addition, in this chapter you'll pick up some new methods to help you position yourself on the cutting edge of the twenty-first century's information explosion.

Unit 18

Fiction

We see then how far the monuments of wit and learning are more durable than the monuments of power, or of the hands. For have not the verses of Homer continued for twenty-five hundred years, or more, without the loss of a syllable or letter; during which time infinite palaces, temples, castles, and cities have ben decayed and demolished?

—*Francis Bacon*

Publishers want you to pick up their novel or short story, so they give you what you need to be an educated consumer. It's all right up front, too, in plain sight! You can use these marketing tools to learn how to power read fiction.

You *Can* Tell a Book by Its Cover!

How do publishers get you to buy and read their latest books? How do they convince you to select one book over another? The main way is through the book's *cover*. As the heading for this section suggests, you *can* learn a great deal about a book without even reading it—just by looking at its cover. Check out the *graphics, colors, letter style,* and *overall design*. Take a few moments to look at the *title, writer, publisher,* and *reviewers' comments*. For example, if the writer has a good reputation, you know that the book will be worth serious consideration. If you have read other books by the writer and enjoyed them, then this particular book might be a book worth a perusal as well. Likewise, look for books published by reputable companies; they give you the best chance of spending your valuable reading time constructively. Then, skim the reviewers' comments on the back cover. Of course, only positive comments will be included, so zero in on who the reviewers are and what they are saying. If the reviewers are well known and have written books that you liked, then the book you are considering is worth looking into more closely.

Take a Look Inside

If the cover of a novel or a collection of short stories catches your interest, it's time to take a look inside. Do a quick preview by checking the *writer's style*. Select a few paragraphs at random and skim them. Get a "taste" of the book!

Skip Descriptive Passages

So you have checked out the cover and the inside of the novel and you've decided that the book appeals to you. However, you just don't have enough time to get through the book. What can you do? Here's a technique that will enable you to read the book in less time.

If a novel has many chapters or a short story is more than a few pages long, it is likely that the characters and setting are described in great detail. You can check this by looking for lots of descriptive words, words that tell *how much? how many? what color? what size?* and *what shape?* If there is a lot of description, consider skimming through these passages or skipping them altogether. You will still get the gist of the story but will be able to get through the plot more quickly. Then slow down the pace when you get to especially suspenseful places in the plot. Follow these steps:

Power Reading Strategy

1. Read the first sentence in the paragraph.

2. Skim the paragraph to see if it contains important plot details.

3. If it does, slow down and pick up the details. If it doesn't, skip over it.

4. Key in on the crucial details.

As you read, keep your focus on the main events of the plot. Be sure to distinguish between characters and see what effect the setting plays on the story's mood. This will help you savor the author's style as well as understand the writer's main idea.

Rereading—Do's and Don'ts!

By this point in the book, you've learned to read faster and better. But with these new skills come temptations! When you're reading with power, you may overlook certain words, phrases, and even sentences. Previous chapters recommend that you do so to get through descriptions in novels more quickly! When this happens, you may decide to look back over the text. "How else can I be sure I caught everything the author wrote?" you may say. "I have to go back to pick up what I missed."

In some cases, you're right. If you've overlooked something especially important to the plot or characterization, you are best served by rereading specific passages. It harms your comprehension to misunderstand the setting or misinterpret the point of view. But looking back over the text too often can become a bad reading habit.

Recall that you learned that you do not have to read every word to understand a novel or a short story. With these types of writing, it is not difficult at all to catch the author's meaning from the whole. By reading key words and phrases, in most cases you can easily catch the author's meaning and the flavor of the book. You don't have to read every single word.

Try these steps to help you avoid rereading unnecessary words and phrases.

Power Reading Strategy

1. As you read, mark any confusing passages.

2. Keep reading! See if reading gives you the answers you need.

3. If you're still confused, go back over the marked passages when you're all done reading an entire chapter.

Exercise

Below is a story by Edgar Allan Poe. Read the story in two sessions, using some of the power reading techniques you learned in this lesson and previously in the book. Since this story doesn't have a cover, you can't preview the graphics, colors, letter style, and overall design—but you can preview the writer. Think about what you already know about Edgar Allan Poe.

◆ When did he write? In the nineteenth century? In the twentieth century?

◆ Which of Poe's short stories and poems have you already read?

◆ What is his reputation? Why is his writing famous? Why do people read his stories?

Recall that Edgar Allan Poe is a nineteenth-century master of horror stories and detective tales. He is also well known for his poetry and literary criticism. Now skim the first paragraph of the story to preview Poe's writing style. Which words best describe it? Did you say descriptive, ornate, or dense?

Since Poe uses a lot of description, you can slash your reading time—without affecting your enjoyment—by following the steps outlined above: Read the first sentence in the paragraph. Then skim the paragraph to see if it contains important plot details; if it does, slow down and pick up the details. If it doesn't, skip over it. Key in on the crucial details. Try these steps now. Don't forget to time yourself and record your reading rate.

The Black Cat

by Edgar Allan Poe

For the most wild yet most homely narrative which I am about to pen, I neither expect nor solicit belief. Mad indeed would I be to expect it, in a case where my very senses reject their own evidence. Yet, mad I am not—and very surely I do not dream. But tomorrow I die, and today I would unburden my soul. My immediate purpose is to place before the world plainly, succinctly, and without comment, a series of mere household events. In their consequences, these events have terrified—have tortured—have destroyed me. Yet I will not attempt to expound them. To me, they have presented little but horror—to many they will seem less terrible than *baroques*. Hereafter, perhaps some intellect may be found which will reduce my phantasm to the commonplace—some intellect more calm, more logical, and far less excitable than my own, which will perceive, in the circumstances I detail with awe, nothing more than an ordinary succession of very natural causes and effects.

From my infancy I was noted for the docility and humanity of my disposition. My tenderness of heart was even so conspicuous as to make me the jest of my companions. I was especially fond of animals, and was indulged by my parents with a great variety of pets. With these I spent most of my time, and never was so happy as when feeding and caressing them. This peculiarity of character grew with my growth, and, in my manhood, I derived from it one of my principal sources of pleasure. To those who have cherished an affection for faithful and sagacious dog, I need hardly go to the trouble of explaining the nature of the intensity of the gratification thus derived. There is something in the unselfish and self-sacrificing love of a brute, which goes directly to the heart of him who had had the frequent occasion to test the paltry friendship and gossamer fidelity of mere *Man*.

I married early, and was happy to find in my wife a disposition not uncongenial with my own. Observing my partiality for domestic pets, she lost no opportunity of procuring those of the most agreeable kind. We had birds, gold-fish, a fine dog, rabbits, a small monkey, and a *cat*.

This latter was a remarkably large and beautiful animal, entirely black, and sagacious to an astonishing degree. In speaking of his intelligence, my wife, who at heart was not a little tinctured with superstition, made frequent allusion to the ancient popular notion, which regarded all black cats as witches in disguise. Not that she was *serious* upon this point—and I mention the matter at all for no better reason than that it happens, just now, to be remembered.

Pluto—this was the cat's name—was my favorite pet and playmate. I alone fed him, and he attended me wherever I went about the house. It was with difficulty that I could prevent him from following me through the streets.

Our friendship lasted, in this manner, for several years, during which my general temperament and character—through the instrumentality of the Fiend Intemperance—had (I blush to confess it) experienced a radical alteration for the worse. I grew, day by day, more moody, more irritable, more regardless of the feelings of others. I suffered myself to use intemperate language to my wife. At length, I even offered her personal violence. My pets, of course, were made to feel the change in my disposition. For Pluto, I still retained sufficient regard for him to restrain me from maltreating him, as I made no scruple of maltreating the rabbits, the monkey, or even the dog, when, by accident, or through affection, they came in my way. But my disease grew upon me—for what disease is like Alcohol!—and at length even Pluto began to experience some of the effects of my ill temper.

One night, returning home, much intoxicated, from one of my haunts about town, I fancied that the cat avoided my presence. I seized him; when, in his fright at my violence, he inflicted a slight wound upon my hand with his teeth. The fury of a demon instantly possessed me. I knew myself no longer. My original soul seemed. at once to take its flight from my body; and a more than fiendish malevolence, gin-nurtured, thrilled every fiber of my frame. I took from my waistcoat pocket a penknife, opened it, grasped the poor beast by the throat, and deliberately cut one of its eyes from the socket! I blush, I burn, I shudder, while I pen the damnable atrocity.

When reason returned with the morning—when I had slept off the fumes of the night's debauch—I experienced a sentiment half of horror, half of remorse, for the crime of which I had been guilty; but it was, at best, a feeble and equivocal feeling, and the soul remained untouched. I again plunged into excess, and soon drowned in wine all memory of the deed.

In the meantime the cat slowly recovered. The socket of the lost eye presented, it is true, a frightful appearance, but he no longer appeared to suffer any pain. He went about the house as usual, but, as might be expected, fled in extreme terror at my approach. I had so much of my old heart left, as to be at first grieved by this evident dislike on the part of a creature which had once so loved me. But this feeling soon gave way to irritation. And then it came, as if to me final and irrevocable overthrow the spirit of PERVERSENESS. Who has not, a hundred times, found himself committing a vile or stupid action, for no other reason than because he knows he should *not*? This spirit of perverseness, I say, came to my final overthrow. It was this unfathomable longing of the soul to *vex itself*—to offer violence to its own nature—to do wrong for wrong's sake only— that urged me to continue and finally to consummate the injury I had inflicted on the unoffending brute. One morning, in cold blood, I slipped a noose about its neck with the tears streaming from my eyes, and with the bitterest remorse at my heart;—hung it *because* I knew that it had loved me, and *because* I felt it had given me no reason of offense;—hung it *because* I knew that in so doing I was committing a sin—a deadly sin that would so jeopardize my immortal soul as to place it—if such a thing were possible—even beyond the reach of the infinite mercy of the Most Merciful and Most Terrible God.

On the night of the day on which this most cruel deed was done, I was aroused from sleep by the cry of fire. The curtains of my bed were in flames. The whole house was blazing. It was with great difficulty that my wife, a servant, and myself, made our escape from the conflagration. The destruction was complete. My entire worldly wealth was swallowed up, and I resigned myself thenceforward to despair.

On the day succeeding the fire, I visited the ruins. The walls, with one exception, had fallen in. The exception was found in a compartment wall, not very thick, which stood about the middle of the house, and against which rested the head of my bed. I approached and saw, as if graven in *bas-relief* upon the white surface, the figure of a gigantic *cat*. The impression was given with an accuracy truly marvelous. There was a rope about the animal's neck.

When I first beheld this apparition—for I could scarcely regard it as less—my wonder and my terror were extreme. But at length reflection came to my aid. The cat, I remembered, had been hung in a garden adjacent to the house. Upon the alarm of fire, this garden had been immediately filled by the crowd—by some one of whom the animal must have been cut from the tree and thrown, through an open window, into my chamber. This had probably been done with the view of arousing me from sleep. The falling of the other walls had compressed the victim of my cruelty into the substance of the freshly-spread plaster; the lime of which, with the flames, and ammonia from the carcass, had then accomplished the portraiture as I saw it.

Reading Time: _____

Word Count: 1275

Reading Speed: _____

The Black Cat

For months I could not rid myself of the phantasm of the cat; and, during this period, there came back into my spirit a half-sentiment that seemed, but was not, remorse. I went so far as to regret the loss of the animal, and to look about me, among the vile haunts I now habitually frequented, for another pet of the same species, and of somewhat similar appearance, with which to supply its place.

One night as I sat, half stupefied, in a den of more than infamy, my attention was suddenly drawn to some black object, reposing upon the head of one of the immense hogsheads of gin, or rum, which constituted the chief furniture of the apartment. I had been looking steadily at the top of this hogshead for some minutes, and what now caused me surprise was the fact that I had not sooner perceived the object thereupon. I approached it, and touched it with my hand. It was a black cat—a very large one—fully as large as Pluto, and closely resembling him in every aspect but one. Pluto had not a white hair upon any portion of his body; but this cat had a large, though indefinite splotch of white covering nearly the whole region of the breast.

I at once offered the purchase it of the landlord; but this person made no claim to it—knew nothing of it—had never seen it before. When I prepared to go home, the animal evinced a disposition to accompany me. I permitted it to do so; occasionally stopping and patting it as I proceeded. When it reached the house it domesticated itself at once, and became immediately a great favorite of my wife.

For my own part, I soon found a dislike to it arising with me. By slow degrees these feelings of disgust and annoyance rose into the bitterness of hatred. What added, no doubt, to my hatred of the beast was the discovery that, like Pluto, it had been deprived of one of its eyes. With my aversion to this cat, however, its partiality for myself seemed to increase. It followed my footsteps with a pertinacity which it would be difficult to make the reader comprehend. At such times, although I longed to destroy it with a blow, I was yet withheld from so doing, partly by a memory of my former crime, but chiefly—let me confess it at once—by absolute *dread* of it.

My wife had called my attention, more than once, to the character of the mark of white hair, of which I have spoken, and which constitutes the sole visible difference between the strange beast and the one I had destroyed. The reader will remember that this mark, although large, had originally been very indefinite; but, by slow degrees—degrees nearly imperceptible and which for a long time my reason struggled to reject as fanciful—it had, at length, assumed a rigorous distinctness of outline. It was now the representation of an object I shudder to name—and for this, above all, I loathed, and dreaded, and would have rid myself of the monster had I dared—it was now, I say, the image of a hideous —of a ghastly thing—of the GALLOWS! —oh, mournful and terrible engine of Horror and Crime— of Agony and of Death!

Beneath the pressure of torments such as these the feeble remnant of the good within me succumbed. Evil thoughts became my sole intimates—the darkest and most evil thoughts. The moodiness of my usual temper increased to hatred of all things and of all mankind; which from the sudden, frequent, and ungovernable outbursts of a fit to which I now blindly abandoned myself, my uncomplaining wife, alas, was the most usual and patient of sufferers.

One day she accompanied me, upon some household errand, into the cellar of the old building which our poverty compelled us to inhabit. The cat followed me down the steep stairs, and, nearly throwing me headlong, exasperated me to madness. Uplifting an ax, and forgetting in my wrath the childish dread which had hitherto stayed my hand, I aimed a blow at the animal, which, of course, would have proved instantly fatal had it descended as I wished. But this blow was arrested by the hand of my wife. Goaded by the interference into a rage more than demoniac, I withdrew my arm from her grasp and buried the ax in her brain. She fell dead upon the spot without a groan.

This hideous murder accomplished, I set myself forthwith, and with entire deliberation, to the task of concealing the body. I knew that I could not remove it from the house, either by day or by night, without the risk of being observed by the neighbors. Many projects entered my mind. At one period I thought of cutting the corpse into minute fragments, and destroying them by fire. At another, I resolved to dig a grave for it in the floor of the cellar. Again, I deliberated about casting it the well in the yard—about packing it in a box, as if merchandise, with the usual arrangements, and so getting a porter to take it from the house. Finally I hit upon what I considered a far better expedient than either of these. I determined to wall it up in the cellar, as the monks of the Middle Ages are recorded to have walled up their victims.

By means of a crowbar I easily dislodged the bricks, and, having carefully deposited the body against the inner wall, I propped it in that position, while with a little trouble I relaid the whole structure as it originally stood. I prepared a plaster which could not be distinguished from the old, and with this I carefully went over all the new brick-work. When I had finished, I was very satisfied that all was right. The wall did not present the slightest appearance of having been disturbed.

My next step was to look for the beast which had been the cause of so much wretchedness; for I had, at length, firmly resolved to put it to death. It did not make its appearance during the night; and thus for one night, at last, since its inception in the house, I soundly and tranquilly slept; aye, slept even with the burden of murder upon my soul.

The second and third day passed, and still my tormentor came not. Once again I breathed as a free man. The monster, in terror, had fled the premises for ever! I should behold it no more! My happiness was supreme! The guilt of my dark deed disturbed me but little. Some few inquiries had been made but these had been readily answered. Even a search had been instituted—but of course nothing was to be discovered. I looked upon my future felicity as secured.

Upon the fourth day of the assassination, a party of the police came, very unexpectedly, into the house, and preceded again to make rigorous investigation of the premises. Secure, however, in the inscrutability of my place of concealment, I felt no embarrassment whatever. The officers bade me accompany them in their search. They left no nook or corner unexplored. At length, they descended to the cellar. My heart beat calmly as that of one who slumbers in innocence. I folded my arms upon my bosom, and roamed easily to and fro. The police were thoroughly satisfied and prepared to depart. The glee at my heart was too strong to be satisfied. I blurted to say but one word by way of triumph, and to render doubly sure their assurance of my guiltless.

"Gentlemen," I said at last, as the party ascended the steps, "I delight to have allayed your suspicions. I wish you all health and a little more courtesy. By the bye, gentlemen, this—this is a very well-constructed house—I may say an excellently well-constructed house.

These walls—are you going, gentlemen?—these walls are solidly put together"; and here, through the mere frenzy of bravado, I rapped heavily with a cane which I held in my hand, upon that very portion of the brickwork behind which stood the corpse of the wife of my bosom.

But may God shield and deliver me from the fangs of the Arch-Fiend! No sooner had the reverberation of my blows sunk into silence, than I was answered by a voice from within the tomb!—by a cry, at first muffled and broken, like the sobbing of a child, and then quickly swelling into one long, loud, and continuous scream, utterly anomalous and inhuman—a howl—a wailing shriek, half of horror and half of triumph, such as might have arisen only out of hell, conjointly from the throats of the damned in their agony and of the demons that exult in the damnation.

Of my own thoughts it is folly to speak. Swooning, I staggered to the opposite wall. For one instant the party on the stairs remained motionless, through extremity of terror and awe. In the next a dozen stout arms were toiling at the wall. It fell bodily. The corpse, already greatly decayed and clotted with gore, stood erect before the eyes of the spectators. Upon its head, with red extended mouth and solitary eye of fire, sat the hideous beast whose craft had seduced me into murder, and whose informing voice had consigned me to the hangman. I had walled up the monster within the tomb.

Reading Time: _____
Word Count: 1400
Reading Speed: _____

Suggested Reading

Below is a list of interesting novels and short stories you may want to read as you practice the power reading techniques you have learned. We do not pretend to include an exhaustive list but simply to suggest some books that will entertain and educate you.

Popular Fiction

Secrets of the Morning by V. C. Andrews

The Hunt for Red October by Tom Clancy

All Around the Town by Mary Higgins Clark

Disclosure by Michael Crichton

The Waterworks by E. L. Doctorow

The Firm by John Grisham

The Silence of the Lambs by Thomas Harris

Misery by Stephen King

Hideaway by Dean Koontz

Scruples by Judith Krantz

The Bourne Supremacy by Robert Ludlum

Centennial by James A. Michener

Interview with the Vampire by Anne Rice

The Stars Shine Down by Sidney Sheldon

Jewels by Danielle Steele

The Joy Luck Club by Amy Tan

Classic Fiction

Pride and Prejudice by Jane Austen

Jane Eyre by Charlotte Brontë

Wuthering Heights by Emily Brontë

A Clockwork Orange by Anthony Burgess

Under Western Eyes by Joseph Conrad

Crime and Punishment by Fyodor Dostoevski

An American Tragedy by Theodore Dreiser

Invisible Man by Ralph Ellison

Light in August by William Faulkner

The Great Gatsby by F. Scott Fitzgerald

Madame Bovary by Gustave Flaubert

The Lord of the Flies by William Golding

The Power and the Glory by Graham Greene

The Return of the Native by Thomas Hardy

The Scarlet Letter by Nathaniel Hawthorne

Catch-22 by Joseph Heller

A Farewell to Arms by Ernest Hemingway

The Turn of the Screw by Henry James

Dubliners by James Joyce

Sons and Lovers by D. H. Lawrence

The Call of the Wild by Jack London

Moby Dick by Herman Melville

Song of Solomon by Toni Morrison

In a Free State by V. S. Naipaul

The Short Stories of Flannery O'Connor by Flannery O'Connor

Animal Farm by George Orwell

The Bell Jar by Sylvia Plath

The Catcher in the Rye by J. D. Salinger

The Grapes of Wrath by John Steinbeck

War and Peace by Leo Tolstoy

The Adventures of Huckleberry Finn by Mark Twain

The Accidental Tourist by Anne Tyler

Rabbit, Run by John Updike

To the Lighthouse by Virginia Woolf

Native Son by Richard Wright

Nonfiction

What about reading *nonfiction* for pleasure? So far, we've concentrated on reading nonfiction for on-the-job responsibilities, but nonfiction can also be a good source of pleasure reading. Many people enjoy reading essays, biographies, and autobiographies for relaxation. Here are ways to help you make the most of the leisure time you have for reading.

Check the Introductory Material

When you pick out a nonfiction book, preview it just as you would a novel or collection of short stories. Take a look at the *preface,* an introductory essay about the book, subject, and author. See if you recognize the author of the preface. If it's a well-known person in the field, it is likely that the book has been carefully written. The preface can also give you valuable hints about the contents of the book, its biases, and its structure.

Then take a few minutes to skim the *introduction.* Since it outlines the book's structure, it can also help you briefly analyze the author's writing style. Check the level of diction (word use) and look for the author's bias. Based on this preview, decide if it's a book that you want to read.

One of the most important parts of any nonfiction book is the *Table of Contents.* Consider it a road map that gives you the lay of the land. Look at the introductory and final chapters and the method of organization. This can help you decide which chapters to read. Sometimes a table of contents will be *annotated.* This means that every chapter will be followed by a brief description of its contents. This is an invaluable aid for a power reader because it can save you the time of previewing the chapters. All you have to do is skim these annotations.

Exercise

Preview the table of contents below. Then answer the questions that follow.

How Fair Is the Nation's Tax Burden?

1. What information will you find in Chapter 1?

_____

2. Where can you find facts about new taxation laws?

_____

3. What is the source of most local funding?

_____

4. Are all states taxed equally? Where did you get this information?

_____

5. What has made the federal tax system regressive?

_____

Answers

   1. How statistics can be used to skew the issue of fairness in taxation

   2. Chapter 2

   3. Property taxes

   4. No; Chapter 4

   5. Payroll taxes, which apply at a fixed rate to all earned income up to a specified cutoff

Check the Back Pages of a Book

Let's take a look now at some of the ways you can use the information in the end matter of a book to help you read faster and better. Start with the *glossary,* a list of technical terms used in the text. Previewing the glossary can give you information about the book's depth and level of difficulty. Skim through the words. See how many you know—and how many you need to learn.

Then look for *endnotes.* See how many endnotes are listed at the back of the book and their sources. Is the author drawing from well-known writers and authoritative texts in the field? If so, the book is likely one that will give you important, valid information—and so be enjoyable to read for its content as well as its style.

Reading Ahead: Do's and Don'ts!

You have learned that rereading can be helpful under very specific circumstances. Rereading when it is not necessary, however, can impede both speed and comprehension. What about the opposite problem—reading ahead?

Reading ahead is not the same as previewing a text, the power reading technique you just learned. Reading ahead while you are reading only serves to cut back on speed without adding comprehension. The temptation to read ahead can be great, but resist it! Use the following guidelines to avoid reading ahead.

◆ Preview the front matter. Look at the copyright date, preface, introduction, and table of contents.

◆ Preview the back matter. Look at the glossary, endnotes, and index.

◆ Be sure that you understand the material you have previewed.

◆ Since you will already know what comes next in the book, you will be less likely to read ahead.

Autobiographies and Biographies

Autobiographies and biographies are common types of nonfiction that people read for pleasure. An *autobiography* is a nonfiction account of a person's life written by the subject. As such, it describes key events from the person's life and is usually written in the first person (using the pronoun *I*). A *biography* is a nonfiction account of a person's life written by another person. Biographies are often written about well-known, important, influential or infamous people.

Read the following excerpt of a biography of Abraham Lincoln by Walt Whitman. Use the power reading techniques described above. Preview the text to avoid reading ahead.

August 12th

I see the President almost every day, as I happen to live where he passes to or from his lodging out of town. He never sleeps at the White House during the hot season, but has quarters at a health location some three miles north of the city, the Soldiers' home, a United States military establishment. I saw him this morning about 8:30 coming into business, riding on Vermont Avenue, near L Street. He always has a company of twenty-five or thirty cavalry, with sabers drawn and held upright over their shoulders....

Mr. Lincoln on the saddle generally rides a good-sized, easy-going gray horse, is dressed in plain black, somewhat rusty and dusty, wears a stiff black hat, and looks about as ordinary in attire, etc., as the commonest man....I see very plainly Abraham Lincoln's dark brown face, with the deep-cut lines, the eyes, always to me with a deep latent sadness in the expression....We have got so that we exchange bows, and very cordial ones.

Part 9

Power Reading Review

Now it's time to pull together everything that you have learned. Use all your power reading techniques as you read the following passages. Work as quickly as you can, but don't sacrifice comprehension. Time yourself to calculate reading speed.

Passage 1: Electronic Publishing

The key to this configuration is to purchase products that adhere to or promote the use of international, national, or government standards as well as industry-standard hardware and software. Use of these products facilitates the use of off-the-shelf components and system extensibility as well as the ability to achieve a seamless integrated environment. These products, often called Fourth Wave systems, encompass application software programs, input and output devices, computer systems, networking, and information management and data exchange services. Examples of standards used in Fourth Wave systems are listed in Figure 1.

System Components: Functionality

In addition to configuring the system components, the system integrator must ensure that the system will consist of all the appropriate and necessary components. In fact, the success of performing a publishing task and achieving the desired results depends on this.

For example, to include a black-and-white photograph in a document, not only is a grayscale scanner needed, but also:

◆ software to manipulate the pixels of the scanned image, in order to clean up or enhance the image

◆ software that understands the format of the image

◆ a high-resolution monitor that can distinguish the different levels of gray

◆ sufficient memory in the computer system to store and process the image

◆ an output device with sufficient memory to represent the document with the embedded image and that can produce continuous tone output (e.g., phototypesetter)

Figure 1

Component	Standard
Operating System	POSIX, DOS, VMS, UNIX, Macintosh
Data Interchange and Data Formats	SGML, ODA/ODIF, CGM, GKS, IGES, ASCII, TIFF, PCX, WKS (Lotus 1-2-3)
Database Access	SQL
Data Communications	OSI, TCP/IP, SNA, DECNET
Network File Access	NFS, RFS
User Interface	Xwindows, Microsoft Windows, GEM, Macintosh

Time and effort should be spent to ensure that the publishing system will perform the necessary functions. Start by reviewing each component's specifications and requirements and plan to configure the system accordingly. A demonstration of the components and system is helpful in knowing which components are necessary and how they work together. Moreover, a demonstration provides assurances that the desired results are attainable.

Reading Time: _____

Word Count: 390

Reading Speed: _____

Passage 2: Sleep Disorders

Sleep disorders are common and often serious. Conservatively speaking, ten to twenty percent of the population have chronic sleep problems. First, some background about normal sleep. There are three distinct states of being that relate to our understanding of normal sleep: wakefulness and *two* states of sleep that are as different from each other as sleep in general is different from wakefulness. They are rapid eye movement (REM) sleep and non-rapid eye movement (non-REM) sleep. Let's take a look at these two forms of sleep.

REM Sleep

Rapid eye movement sleep is much more like wakefulness than non-REM sleep. For example, the EEG of a person in REM sleep is a fast, low-voltage recording that looks like the tracing of a person who is wide awake. This indicates that the brain is very active during REM sleep; that's when the majority of dreaming occurs. So there are active mental processes during REM sleep. Arguably, the brain is more active during REM sleep than it is when we are wide awake.

Rapid eye movement occurs during REM sleep—hence the name; but most skeletal muscles throughout the body are paralyzed during REM sleep. Obviously, the muscles of respiration are spared, but the arms and legs are flaccid during REM sleep. As when we're awake, there is a high degree of autonomic nervous system activity during REM sleep. This is manifested by variable blood pressure, respiration, and pulse.

Non-REM Sleep

Non-REM sleep is exhibited by very different symptoms. It's a quiet state, both physically and mentally. The majority of sleep is non-REM sleep. All non-REM sleep produces a slow EEG, but it can be divided into four stages, based on the degree of EEG slowing: Stages 3 and 4 exhibit the greatest slowing and together are called "slow-wave" sleep, which is the deepest stage of non-REM sleep. This is the form of sleep in which the individual is the most deeply asleep and the most difficult to arouse.

A Twenty-five-hour Cycle

Sleep is part of a twenty-four-hour cycle, or, more correctly, a twenty-*five*-hour cycle. It turns out that people are naturally programmed for a twenty-five-hour day, a fact established in many experiments in which individuals are kept in environments with no time cues. The subjects are usually graduate students working on theses who don't mind being cooped up for weeks or months without windows, clocks, or any sense of time in the outside world. Within two or three days, these individuals gradually shift their daily schedules. They go to bed later and get up later as they begin to follow a twenty-five-hour cycle, spending about one third of the time asleep and two thirds of it awake.

Because we are programmed to live on a twenty-five-hour cycle (despite conforming to a solar cycle of twenty-four hours), it's difficult to force ourselves to go to bed and to awaken when we should. It can be particularly difficult after a weekend of following the natural instinct to fall asleep later and arise later when, on Monday, we have to go back to the rhythms of the solar day and to societal conventions.

Almost every aspect of physiology has some kind of circadian rhythm. We have long known that the temperature of the body varies independently of activity and ambient temperature. For example, if a person is doing the same thing at midnight and at noon, and the room temperature is unchanged, the person's body will be cooler at night. Almost every aspect of bodily function has some variations around the clock. The sleep-wake cycle is the dominant rhythm of the body, and all other rhythms are linked to it. Following the disruption of the sleep-wake cycle, it may take several weeks before these various internal rhythms once again become synchronized.

Reading Time: _____

Word Count: 550

Reading Speed: _____

Passage 3: Preparing for Climate Change

Uncertainty about where, when, or how much climate change will occur makes preparing for its impacts both difficult and essential, according to the Congressional Office of Technology Assessment (OTA) in a Summary Report released today.

However, what the federal government decides now about the management of water supplies, forests, wetlands, fish, wildlife, and natural resources could limit or foreclose the ability of these resources and their managers to adapt to changing climate conditions or could help us better prepare, says the OTA. Delay in taking action, warns OTA, may leave the nation poorly prepared for the changes ahead and may increase the possibility of irreversible impacts or costly surprises. Many of the options OTA presents could address problems already facing those natural resources and could be undertaken regardless of how the climate might change.

The ambitious $1.4 billion U.S. Global Change Program (USGCP) is predominantly a physical science program aimed at observing, understanding, and predicting climate change. As currently structured, it will not provide decision makers and natural resource managers with the information they will need to respond to climate change.

The recent major drought in the western and southeastern United States, powerful hurricanes in Florida, and substantial flooding in the Midwest represent the types of extreme events that may occur with greater frequency if the climate warms.

Predicated climate changes include increased temperatures, rising sea levels, changing patterns of precipitation, and increased evaporation. Combined, these factors could significantly alter the nation's natural resources. Resulting loss of soil moisture might prevent the greatest threat to natural systems.

Sea-level rise could increase the erosion of shorelines and accelerate loss of coastal wetlands. Changes in precipitation could lead to more floods and droughts and disruption of water supplies. In regions that become drier, interior wetlands could be lost. The ideal ranges for plants and animals might shift hundreds of miles north as temperatures increase. Shifts in the range of agricultural crops and commercial tree species could lead to disruptions in rural communities. More frequent fire and die-back may occur in forests stranded outside their ideal climate range.

Since the 1992 United Nations Conference on Environment and Development (UNCED), more than 160 countries have signed the Climate Convention, seeking to freeze greenhouse gas emissions at 1990 levels in the near future. The United States has just announced its plan to return to the 1990 emissions levels by the year 2000. However, even under the most optimistic future emissions scenarios, average global temperatures are expected to increase several degrees over the next century as a result of past emissions.

OTA examines the ability of natural resource-based systems to adapt to climate change and considers means to enhance adaptation by modifying management, advancing research and technology, disseminating information, and taking legislative action. OTA focused on areas where future costs may be very high; impacts may be irreversible; the validity of long-term decisions made today will be affected; preparing for catastrophic events is already warranted and a significant federal role exists in research, planning, or management of these systems.

On the basis of this focus, OTA selected six systems for future analysis: coastal areas, water resources, agriculture, wetlands, preserves (federally protected natural areas), and forests. Each of these systems is stressed to some degree today, says OTA, and that may influence how well it can respond to any future climate change. For example, because populations in coastal areas are growing, the exposure to costly natural disaster is increasing.

OTA groups policy options to four themes shared by several or all systems: geographical and institutional fragmentation; inadequate communication of climate risk; lack of contingency planning to prepare for extreme events or weather surprises; and information gaps in various key scientific and policy areas. OTA considers more than a hundred options in the full report.

Any policies that improve the chances of adapting to climate change more smoothly and painlessly provide buffers against its negative impacts, notes OTA. Of benefit are flexible policies that improve our abilities to make quick self-adjustments or midcourse corrections as needed without major economic or social disruption. OTA also suggests actions necessary to ensure that the nation is prepared to cope with the potential for serious threats to its natural resources.

Reading Time: _____

Word Count: 780

Reading Speed: _____